Whatever Happened to the Rich Young Man?

Whatever Happened to the Rich Young Man?

The Church and the New Marginalized

KEITH FOSTER

WIPF & STOCK · Eugene, Oregon

WHATEVER HAPPENED TO THE RICH YOUNG MAN?
The Church and the New Marginalized

Copyright © 2020 Keith Foster. All rights reserved. Except for brief quotations in critical publications or reviews, no part of this book may be reproduced in any manner without prior written permission from the publisher. Write: Permissions, Wipf and Stock Publishers, 199 W. 8th Ave., Suite 3, Eugene, OR 97401.

Wipf & Stock
An Imprint of Wipf and Stock Publishers
199 W. 8th Ave., Suite 3
Eugene, OR 97401

www.wipfandstock.com

PAPERBACK ISBN: 978-1-5326-9343-4
HARDCOVER ISBN: 978-1-5326-9344-1
EBOOK ISBN: 978-1-5326-9345-8

Manufactured in the U.S.A. 09/02/20

I dedicate this book to every Christ-follower
who desires to make a difference in the sphere of
influence in which King Jesus has placed them.

Contents

Acknowledgments		ix
Introduction		xi
Chapter 1	The New Marginalized	1
Chapter 2	The Squeaky Wheel Gets the Oil: The Welfare-Dominated Church	9
Chapter 3	Negotiating the Third Place	16
Chapter 4	Café Ethnography: A Unique Opportunity	26
Chapter 5	A Tale of Two Cafés, Part 1: The Friendship Café	35
Chapter 6	A Tale of Two Cafés, Part 2: The Welcome Café	52
Chapter 7	Theological Reflection and Conclusions	66
Appendix: Questions for Reflection		73
Bibliography		79

Acknowledgments

I would like to acknowledge the input of the staff and volunteers of both The Friendship Café and The Welcome Café into some of the research findings taken from fieldwork. I would also like to acknowledge the helpful feedback and editing work of Becky Tucker.

Introduction

The idea for this book came out of my doctoral studies at Roehampton University, London. For a long time, I had been frustrated by (what I saw) as the church's focus on the needy within the local community, with its resources and programs often being dominated by this demographic. As someone who had both volunteered and served in a paid role for the church in (what was defined as) a "deprived area," I appreciated the importance of such a "service of mercy." Additionally, as an evangelical Christian, I had a clear biblical understanding of God's heart for the poor, the widow, the vulnerable; but what about those who were "well off" or just "doing okay"? What about those who did not have any obvious needs, yet all the same needed Christ, needed to know the life-saving message of the life, death, resurrection, and return of King Jesus? The church I was serving in (at the time) had no "program" for them.

My own experience working in industry, both corporate and military, for twenty-five years, the last ten in senior management, had also reaffirmed the problem. Outside of inviting people to church, by and large the church had no intentional strategy to reach what I call the New Marginalized, those without obvious economic needs. As I worked in various roles in various companies (e.g., operations manager, project manager, company owner), I felt a disconnect between the high-flying corporate world with its company cars, hospitality, and multi-million-pound projects, and my low-budget, occasionally dysfunctional church. How on earth could the church (not just the one I attended, but the many who struggled to

Introduction

connect with the corporate world) even begin to relevantly reach out to the New Marginalized?

This sense of disconnect was only confirmed when I took up the senior pastorate of Bethel Church in Coventry in 2009. The church was one of eighty-eight churches planted between 1928 and 1937, and the last church to be planted out of the Bethel evangelical tent campaign.[1] The church was located between two very different and contrasting areas, one considered deprived and the other affluent and somewhat metropolitan. The church had a busy and efficient program, all run by enthusiastic volunteers, yet by and large with a focus on the welfare demographic. The conversations around any outreach were largely directed at "those over in the flats" and those with drug and alcohol addictions—the obvious needy. Several members in professional roles had expressed frustration at this strategy: What about their friends and work colleagues? What could be done to reach them? Ministry in the workplace was rarely spoken of in the main, even ignored. Within my first year, I delivered a short series of studies on ministry in the workplace using some helpful materials produced by the London Institute of Contemporary Christianity (LICC). However, this was a token offering. The general focus and outreach culture of the church was geared toward the welfare demographic, the measured marginalized. Something needed to be done. The more people I spoke to, the more common I found this problem to be: Professional people in churches who were happy to serve and tithe for the Kingdom somehow felt a disconnect between the church and their corporate lives. Thus, this book.

THIS BOOK

Whatever Happened to the Rich Young Man? has been born out of this frustration. Yet this is not simply a book that laments the (already) well-rehearsed issue of a disconnect with the New Marginalized, the non-welfare demographic; but one that is written to encourage church leaders and everyday members to make those

1. Watts, *Edward Jefferies*.

Introduction

connections. As a mix of theology, personal anecdote, and practical case studies (ones I have had the pleasure to be involved with), this book seeks to encourage the church to "broaden its nets," to be inspired to think beyond its stereotyped role as a neoliberal welfare provider, and to recognize that we are all spiritually needy. As the "hope of the world," the church is best placed to reach (what Jesus referred to as) the "impossible" (Luke 18:18–30).

Keith Foster
May 2020

Chapter 1

The New Marginalized

Ron was a well-presented, seasoned businessman. And a successful one, at that. As the managing director of a national tire distribution company, Ron had a reputation for being a ruthless, no-nonsense kind of guy. At the time, I worked for a national car fleet company as their operations manager. Part of my role was to negotiate the tire deals for our forty thousand vehicles located across the country. I enjoyed negotiating with clients within an industry renowned for generous hospitality. One such negotiation happened during a five-star weekend in Barcelona. Several multi-national decision makers came on the trip, including Ron. More about Ron and Barcelona later.

I had become a Christian at the age of sixteen. Between the ages of fourteen and sixteen, I visited my uncle and his family in Newark, UK, and I had always noticed something different about them. I later found that "something" to be Jesus. One summer, my uncle shared the gospel with me. I instantly knew that I needed forgiveness—a new direction. In August 1979, I asked Christ not only to save my life for eternity but to help me follow him into whatever he had for me. That "whatever" would lead (a year later) to joining the military. By the age of twenty-one, I had encountered two combat situations. During this time, I met a local girl (Lesley) on

Whatever Happened to the Rich Young Man?

leave in my home city (Hull, UK) and soon we were married. Lesley was God-fearing but had never heard the gospel of salvation and allegiance to a new master, King Jesus. During our time in military married quarters, we started to attend a local Baptist church where Lesley heard the gospel preached for the first time. My wife became a sister in Christ, too. From that point, we were always seeking God's purposes for us. Having sensed a call to ministry very early in my "walk" with Christ, this would often become the topic of our conversations about the future. We were to learn that the Lord is never in a rush, with the path to His purposes often being "long and windy" as he shapes us through our faltering commitment, obedience, and circumstances. This included being led out of the military in 1989 to take up a junior role in a local shipbuilding company. The character of Joseph in the book of Genesis had long been a hero of mine. How had he remained consistent in his faith, despite the injustices and seeming "slow progress" of God's purposes for him? I saw a parallel in my preparation for service, which included eight years working for the shipbuilding company, leading to a management role and college education in business and finance. After having had some eighteen years in the defense industry by then, I needed a change. It was then in 1997 that I secured a senior role with a large, national car fleet company.

All this time, I had faithfully been serving at that local Baptist church. The people were friendly and hospitable and the social life was good. However, there seemed to be a huge disconnect between this "sacred space" and the Monday-to-Friday "secular space" where I spent most of my time. At church, nobody spoke about our "secular spaces," with the reverse being true in my workplace. Yet since I came to know Christ, I had a passion and desire to share and communicate my faith, whatever arena or "space" wherein I found myself. Yet all the time I felt isolated, like some sort of Christian vigilante that God had sent into the challenging corporate world. Perhaps Jesus was right when he said it was "impossible" for the rich to enter the Kingdom of Heaven (Luke 18:18–27). Yet the story of the rich young man has often been misunderstood, with Jesus being misquoted as declaring it "impossible" for the rich to enter the Kingdom of God. I too had misread the whole Lukan narrative in chapter 18. Reading on, I read about Zacchaeus (the well-off tax collector) who encountered Christ and about whom Jesus could subsequently announce, "Salvation has come to this house today" (Luke 19:9). There was hope for Ron yet.

So, back to Barcelona. It had been a long day of negotiating and discussing. Everyone was tired and needed an early night for another full day of negotiations the next day. Ron had said he was going to go for a walk along the beautiful Barcelona harbor, laden with multi-million-pound yachts, boats, and private gin palaces. The backdrop could not have been more corporate and lavish as Ron and I strolled along the harbor front together. Exhausted from the day's corporate conversation, we were both keen to simply chat about life, family, and world news. Ron had asked about my family situation, additionally asking what I did when I wasn't thinking about work. I told him about my leadership role in my church and shared my faith story about how it all started. Ron was polite but gave no real signs of immediate interest. I asked Ron about his family and hobbies. Ron proceeded to tell me about the challenges of home. He and his wife had an only child who was disabled and needed constant care. That was my opportunity. Silently praying for wisdom and an understanding reception, I said to Ron, "I am going to pray for your daughter and family." Ron burst into tears. This tough (on the outside) negotiator, who radiated self-sufficiency, had a spiritual vulnerability—one, I believe, that we all have, yet by and large the church ignores. Perhaps part of the reason is the cosmetic "myth" of self-sufficiency communicated by the New Marginalized.

SO WHO ARE THE NEW MARGINALIZED?

The concept of the New Marginalized arose out of my doctoral studies and conversations with two scholars who were already writing about the church's engagement within the local community. Professor Chris Baker (Goldsmiths University, London) and Professor Paul Cloke (Exeter University, UK) have done extensive work and research in two key areas: Baker in the area of the faith community's contribution to social capital, and Cloke in his research around

Whatever Happened to the Rich Young Man?

evangelizing the welfare demographic.[1] I will cover these in more detail in chapter 2; however, a summary of each will suffice here.

For a long time, social scientists have spoken about "social capital," a term used to define how people feel about the places and communities where they live. In my former (joint-authored) book with Andrew Hardy, I gave this a complete treatment.[2] Suffice to say that Baker sees the church as having a valuable contribution to make to that local sense of community. Baker speaks of *religious* and *spiritual* capital as the "what" and "why" of the faith community's local community involvement. Spiritual capital is the motivation or "why" behind what faith-based organizations (FBO) do; religious capital is the actual "what" that they do and the practical form that takes. I found Baker's insights challenging as they encouraged community engagement in local groups and activities, but as an evangelical believing in the need for personal and community transformation, community engagement with a gospel-centered intentionality was also needed. Cloke (as an evangelical) addressed this with regard to community engagement with the vulnerable. His challenging work around evangelizing the vulnerable (including the ethic of such) provided another research marker for me. As a piece of doctoral research, my work would need to be unique in its contribution to both knowledge and practice, especially since my research doctorate was in practical theology.

Positioning my research between Baker and Cloke, I sought to develop a research project that not only contributed to the sense of local community, but did so with a conversionist, gospel-driven agenda. Additionally, while there was a significant amount of research being carried out amongst the measured marginalized, I could not find any amongst those with no obvious and presenting needs. Indeed, the more I read Cloke's and Baker's works, the clearer it became that there was a neglected demographic emerging—the non-welfare. I was reluctant to call this demographic "the rich," as this would be subjective depending upon context. Instead, my focus

1. For example, Baker, *Spiritual Capital and Progressive Localism;* Cloke, Beaumont, and Williams, *Working Faith, Faith-Based Organisations and Urban Social Justice.*

2. Hardy and Foster, *Body and Blood.*

would be on those who did not receive any financial or welfare assistance from the government. I called this group the New Marginalized. The first two years of my preliminary research confirmed my experiential suspicions from my time in the corporate world and currently in the church. There was a demographic of people who were "unmeasured" by national statistic agencies and subsequently ignored by churches and their missional strategies. Yet having had many experiences with people (like the one I had with Ron in Barcelona), I knew that these people had needs, too.

WHY IS IT SO TOUGH?

Luke 18 tells us the account of the rich young man (Luke 18:18–30). In this account, Luke tells us about a ruler who came to Jesus inquiring as to what he needed to do to inherit eternal life. As well as grounding his answer in God's Word [*Torah*], Jesus spoke into the personal cost that was necessary for any would-be follower:

> Sell everything you have and give to the poor, and you will have treasure in heaven. Then, come follow me. (Luke 18:22)

The challenge was too much for this rich young ruler, who, Luke tells us, "went away sad" (Luke 18:23).

Christ's summary to the onlooking disciples was to declare "How hard [*duskolos*] it is for the rich to enter the kingdom of God" (Luke 18:24). The original Greek translation of *duskolos* refers more to the English translation of *difficult*. Over time, as stories are told, meanings can be elaborated. Such is the case in this story, which is often misread to mean *impossible* as opposed to *difficult*. There is a huge difference between something that is difficult and something impossible. Even here in Luke 18, in anticipation of the misunderstanding of the disciples and the story's ongoing transmission, Jesus can assure the disciples that; "What is impossible [*adynata*] with man, is possible [*dynata*] with God" (Luke 18:27). When God is at work in a situation, including someone's heart, this changes *duskolos* or even seemingly *adynata* situations into *dynata* opportunities.

Whatever Happened to the Rich Young Man?

As well as deconstructing the disciple's worldview that imagined riches equal blessing and divine favor, Jesus was demonstrating one of the specific hurdles that the well-off demographic faces when it comes to submission to the King and his Kingdom: their possessions. Somehow, in the ongoing dialogue down the centuries, this has translated from "difficult but possible with God" to "impossible for the rich to enter the kingdom of heaven."

One remedy for this would be for a simple sweep of the scriptures to see that many rich, well-off, or simply hard-working people were recruited amongst God's people for his Kingdom purposes. The chapter divisions in our Bibles do not always help our understanding of the flow of authorial intent. Luke finishes this section by recording Jesus declaring the ultimate cost of establishing God's Kingdom, his death (Luke 18:31–33), while at the same time highlighting the spiritual "blindness" of the disciples to understand what he was saying (Luke 18:34). What is then often the case in the Gospels, Luke then follows a section on spiritual blindness with an account of someone who was physically blind, receiving their sight (Luke 18:35–43). This is then all brought together in the next section when Luke gives the account of a well-off tax collector (Zacchaeus) "seeing" Jesus for who he is, embracing his new King, and welcoming him into his home (Luke 19:1–10).

One striking thing about this idea of reaching the non-welfare demographic (we may use other terms such as self-sufficient, well-off, even comparatively rich) is that this is the *only* demographic that Jesus said was *difficult* to reach. Yet for many people and organizations, the *hard* people and places to reach for the Kingdom are often seen as those living in the local, run-down housing estates or those engaging in substance or alcohol abuse. The next chapter will consider and challenge this overemphasis in more detail; it is sufficient to summarize here that if Jesus considered the well-off and materialistic demographic difficult to reach and spiritually blind, what are we as individuals, and more specifically as churches, doing to reach those in hard places? Responding solely to the measured material needs of the communities around our churches can only result in a narrow approach in our missional or outreach strategy. The well-off, although perhaps difficult to reach, have spiritual needs, too.

The New Marginalized

EVERYBODY NEEDS SOMEBODY

A famous quote from Augustine of Hippo states, "Thou madest us for thyself, O Lord, and our heart is restless, until it rest in thee."[3] Famous songs have espoused the same sentiment and need. Lyrics that suggest *everybody needs somebody, we all need somebody to lean on* resonate across society indiscriminately. The writer of Ecclesiastes succinctly puts it when he writes, "God has set eternity in the human heart" (Ecc 3:11). Yet somehow, we have categorized people. Whole groups and generations are now classed under various sociological and theological terms: postmodern, post-secular, Millennial, Generation Z, etc. With these categories come characteristic definitions which we can summarize and assess, specifically regarding their potential receptiveness to our evangelism. Perhaps they are classified as being suspicious of the grand, corporate story: the meta-narrative that seeks to "explain." While these insights are helpful in partnership with a missiological approach that seeks to contextualize the gospel to "all peoples," underpinning all of this is the Bible's timeless challenge to the church to partner with God in his global mission to reach all peoples from all nations. This great commission sees its culmination when the whole cosmos is brought under the single and sovereign rule of God within a "new heavens and earth," with Christ at the head (Rev 21:1–4). In the meantime, we live in this fragmented world that may well desire but ultimately struggles to realize a world where there is "one humanity." Achieving this aside from God's reconciling project is an impossible task. The people of Babel in Genesis 11 desired to reach their "pinnacle," yet they would only end up with a frustrated, unfinished project (Gen 11:1–9).

Equally, people often like to define themselves, perhaps by presenting themselves to the world as they would like to be seen. Before the global phenomenon known as the internet, the only methods people could use to achieve this were their possessions: the clothes they wore, the cars they drove, and the homes they lived in. These (of course) are still used by many to communicate a sense of success or self-sufficiency, but massively impacting this

3. Augustine, *Confessions*, 5.

Whatever Happened to the Rich Young Man?

whole social "display" has been the rise of the internet and associated social media platforms. Social media filters can assist our false self-portrait. The reality of lonely and tragic lives is often hidden by filtered selfies and stories of indulgence. Behind all of this, the rich man is still sad. The church too can believe and be susceptible to this portrayed narrative of self-sufficiency and contentment. Augustine's quote rings true underneath all of this. A life outside of God is restless until it finds it's rest in him. The writer of Ecclesiastes has already told us why: as those with eternity created in our hearts, we have all been made to know God and to find our fulfillment in a life centered around his ultimate project to reconcile the whole cosmos to himself. As Christ-followers and as local churches, it is time to stop believing the projected narrative of self-sufficiency and to constantly keep in mind that *everybody needs somebody*—that somebody being Christ the Redeemer.

Chapter 2

The Squeaky Wheel Gets the Oil: The Welfare-Dominated Church

The importance of looking out and caring for the most vulnerable amongst us is a value, and thus a "metric," that lies at the center of any civilized and morally grounded society. Even the most irreligious societies are founded upon the central principles of (at least several of) the Ten Commandments. It is illegal to murder or steal in every society. Additionally, the Bible's teaching on looking after the vulnerable, the widows, the orphans, the marginalized, are also widely embraced and accepted—at least in principle. Fundraising events hosted by celebrities, charity appeals for famine-torn countries, email campaigns to support the local hospice, all vie for our attention. The challenge is what to say "no" to. For Christ-followers, this is amplified further, since they are told "Whoever is kind to the poor lends to the Lord, and he will reward them for what they have done" (Prov 19:17). Plenty of ink has been spilled by authors and theologians with regard to our obligations to the poor. Herein lies the problem. While there are many obvious and basic needs that all should be able to access (food, shelter, etc.), how might we define the "less well-off"? Wealth and possessions are relative and contextual. By that, I mean that the things we possess only hold

Whatever Happened to the Rich Young Man?

their value within a given context and within the balance of our life experiences and inner well-being. Let me explain: For years, my parents struggled to get by. My father was in and out of jobs, and my mother did what she could as a low-wage auxiliary nurse at the local hospital. Until my teens, my parents rented their home from the local government authority. We lived in an area where most people around us had managed to purchase their home; so contextually, for my parents, being able to purchase their home would be a measure of success and relative "wealth." Well, a few years into my military service, my parents did just that. With incentive discounts from the local authority offered to long-term tenants, my parents proudly purchased their home. Sadly, within only a few short years, my father passed away. While my mother had the security and legacy of a long-term home, I remember her saying, as a relatively young widow, "I would rather have an orange box and your father back, as pleased as I am with this home." Against the context of sudden loss and grief, the comparative value of a house had lost its shine and appeal. As I write this chapter, the world is gripped by a global pandemic—COVID-19. Within the current shutdown, many of the possessions and pursuits that people value and allow to dominate their time and attention are off-limits. Stories are emerging of people being released out of critical care centers with new perspectives and insights around the value of "other things": family, friends, mental, and physical well-being, etc. What is valuable to us can change quickly.

Jesus had plenty to say about the things we value. One of his most famous challenges is found in one of his most famous sermons:

> Do not store up for yourselves treasures on earth, where moths and vermin destroy, and where thieves break in and steal. But store up for yourselves treasures in heaven, where moths and vermin do not destroy, and where thieves do not break in and steal. For where your treasure is, there your heart will be also. The eye is the lamp of the body. If your eyes are healthy, your whole body will be full of light. But if your eyes are unhealthy, your whole body will be full of darkness. If then the light within you is darkness, how great is that darkness! No one can serve two

The Squeaky Wheel Gets the Oil: The Welfare-Dominated Church

masters. Either you will hate the one and love the other, or you will be devoted to the one and despise the other. You cannot serve both God and money. (Matt 6:19–24)

Jesus tells us that within and against the Kingdom context, the things we value now will lose their shine. The church is not exempt from the challenge, either. In his appraisal of the seven churches in the book of Revelation, Jesus brings a reality check to the church at Laodicea:

> To the angel of the church in Laodicea write: These are the words of the Amen, the faithful and true witness, the ruler of God's creation. I know your deeds, that you are neither cold nor hot. I wish you were either one or the other! So, because you are lukewarm—neither hot nor cold—I am about to spit you out of my mouth. You say, "I am rich; I have acquired wealth and do not need a thing." But you do not realize that you are wretched, pitiful, poor, blind and naked. I counsel you to buy from me gold refined in the fire, so you can become rich; and white clothes to wear, so you can cover your shameful nakedness; and salve to put on your eyes, so you can see. (Rev 3:14–18)

An impoverished church, blinded to its poverty, is in no position to see the real poverty of the communities and people surrounding it.

EASY PICKINGS: ENTERING OUR COMMUNITIES

It is not surprising to see many churches using the measurable needs within their local community as a platform upon which to serve and minister to it. As it says in the chapter title, the squeaky wheel gets the oil. The UK Office of National Statistics (ONS), and the United States Census Bureau, provide a wide range of data by which our local communities can be measured. Statistics around health, education, employment, income, housing, etc., are collated to create a "league table" of deprivation. Communities can then be categorized as "deprived areas" depending on their "league position." The basic flaw in this sweeping categorization of a community

Whatever Happened to the Rich Young Man?

is that deprivation is a "people" measure and not a geographical one. A 2015 UK local government report states:

> A geographical area is not deprived: it is the circumstances and lifestyles of the people living there that affect its deprivation score. It is important to remember that not everyone living in a deprived area is deprived—and that not all deprived people live in deprived areas.[1]

This can leave whole rafts of people in every community ignored and neglected by the local church as it seeks to respond to the measurable and published needs.

FILLING THE GAP

It then stands to reason that the church, armed with its local data, can swing into action to meet local needs. The benefit of doing so is twofold. Firstly, it can position the church within its community as a key player and stakeholder. In its attempt to recover central ground, the church is (understandably) keen to do this. Secondly, these are often very real and pressing needs—needs that the church is well-positioned to meet. Add to this the backing of a theological mandate to demonstrate the Kingdom within our communities, this seems like an easy gap to fill. The church can put itself back on the local map. Elaine Graham and Stephen Lowe in their book *What Makes a Good City?* affirm the church's central role. They write: "Christianity has been an urban religion since its very beginnings."[2] Baker and Beaumont add:

> The neoliberal turn and the stripping down of the welfare state have returned us to a condition where public charity once again is called upon and charitable welfare has always been a calling of faith-based organizations.[3]

Is this "mission accomplished," or are we missing something? What about the "unmeasured," those I have referred to as the New

---

1. MHCLG, "English Indices of Deprivation."
2. Graham and Lowe, *What Makes a Good City?*, 5.
3. Beaumont and Baker, *Postsecular Cities*, xiii.

The Squeaky Wheel Gets the Oil: The Welfare-Dominated Church

Marginalized, who exist within all our communities? How are their needs being met? In fact, what *are* their needs? Jesus spoke about a level of deprivation that is not measured by any national statistics office, yet one that impacts everyone: that of *spiritual* poverty. Again, within that famous Sermon on the Mount, within the section referred to as the Beatitudes, the very first quality he lists as a characteristic of a Kingdom citizen is "poor in Spirit." Those who are "spiritually bankrupt." They are indeed "happy," or blessed, "for theirs is the Kingdom of Heaven" (Matt 5:3). Here's a simple interpretation: "How happy are those who acknowledge their spiritual bankruptcy and need for Christ, whose values subsequently change, who from that point seek treasures in heaven." While the church can and must fill local welfare needs—both material and social deprivation—there is a deeper, more pressing spiritual need within every heart and community. If not met, it will have eternal consequences. As the value systems within our communities crumble and lose their shine, it is time for the community of God's people to both demonstrate and communicate Kingdom values and Christ-centered allegiance: those things that Jesus told us do not perish, spoil, or fade (Matt 6:19-21).

MORE THAN WELFARE

The church's biblical mandate to minister to the marginalized, vulnerable, and materially poor is well-rehearsed and accepted. To give credit where credit is due, the church (in general) does this well—so much so that it could be understood that this essential "filling" of the welfare gap in response to the holes in governmental safety nets is deemed (by the casual observer) to be the church's central purpose. This caricaturing of the church into a neoliberal welfare provider can only serve to enhance any "imagined boundaries" or irrelevancies of the church that the non-welfare (New Marginalized) perceive to be the case. This can then become a "comfortable" arrangement for all parties: The welfare demographic is grateful to receive help and support; the New Marginalized quietly admiring the "charity" of the church; and the church itself is then happy to

Whatever Happened to the Rich Young Man?

accept its defined place at the table. As long as this remains the collective understanding, all is well. Yet as an evangelical,[4] the centrality of conversionism (i.e., lives transformed in Christ) lies at the heart (or arguably should) of every project. When visible, this can (and often does) develop a hermeneutic of suspicion, and in some cases can cause the church's "place" at the community table to be brought into question. The fear of losing such a privileged place can then lead to one of two responses: for churches to create their own spaces, or to resume their perceived and accepted role.

This gives rise to several questions and challenges that the remainder of this book will seek to answer and demonstrate:

a. Is it possible for the church to unashamedly possess a gospel intentionality yet keep its place at the community table?
b. Can this be achieved in the very heart of our communities, without having to revert to the tactic of creating our own spaces?
c. Can such spaces be created that engage with a much broader demographic, beyond welfare?
d. Can all of this be achieved while maintaining our identity as unashamed Christ-followers and at the same time enhancing and contributing to a sense of local community?

I believe the answer to all these questions is a resounding "Yes!" My doctoral research sought to investigate and personally embed myself into two such projects, whose overall aims and desires were to enhance their local communities, yet do so with a gospel-centered intentionality. I wanted to know what tensions, imagined or otherwise, existed within each project. Spending two years conducting ethnographic research, I wanted to know the answer to other questions, too:

---

4. David Bebbington's classic *Evangelicalism in Modern Britain: A History from the 1730s to the 1980s* outlines the four key tenets of evangelicalism: Conversionism (desire to see lives transformed for Christ), Biblicism (the Bible informing the whole of life), Activism (faith in action), and Crucicentrism (the centrality of the cross).

a. Was there a difference between the "espoused" theology (this is what we say we do) and "operant" theology (this is what we actually do)?
b. Were all church staff on board with the objectives?
c. Did the New Marginalized who frequented the projects perceive any tensions?
d. Is there hope for the rich young man?

The remainder of this book will detail some of my key findings from my research. Yet in order to carry out this important piece of theological research, I needed to look to an academic "friend" from the secular academy for assistance: sociology. I wanted to know if bringing theology and sociology together within a practical theology doctoral project might jointly provide answers to the above questions. I was not disappointed.

Chapter 3

Negotiating the Third Place

It is one thing to understand the need to reach a broader demographic with the message of the life, death, resurrection, and future return of King Jesus. It is quite another to know where to start. Each of us represents Christ as his ambassadors (2 Cor 5:20), and in that sense we are all on the frontline—wherever we find ourselves on a daily basis.[1] Yet there is something powerful about the *collective* witness of God's people together. My research was keen to discover how the local church might create a meaningful *place* to engage the New Marginalized within their communities, maximizing this collective witness. Leslie Newbigin, the great missionary to India and pioneer of what many call the "missional conversation," defined this powerful collective signature as "the hermeneutic of the gospel"—that is, a community characterized by praise, truth, hope, community, mutual concern, and service.[2] Newbigin considered this collective a true hermeneutic or "interpretation" of what it really means to follow Christ and his Kingdom rule. According to

---

1. The London Institute of Contemporary Christianity (LICC), as previously mentioned, also produce some helpful material with regard to our individual responsibility as Christ-followers—*Fruitfulness on the Frontline* being one such resource.

2. Newbigin, *The Gospel in a Pluralist Society*, 227.

Newbigin, there is nothing more powerful than a community of God's people when it wants to demonstrate to a watching world what it truly means to be a child of the King and a citizen of his Kingdom.

So, what might such places look like? What forms might they take? Any such place would need to be welcoming to all. It should preferably be as neutral a place as possible: a meeting ground for friendship, discussion, and social interaction. My interaction with sociology would provide the answer in the form of the *Third Place*.

WHAT ARE THIRD PLACES?

Third Places have been the subject and interest of sociologists, researchers, and "everyday" people for many years. Sociologists and researchers like to study and measure the interactions within Third Places, while everyday people simply like to frequent them. So, what are they? A number of definitions have been offered. Third Places are places that offer "social and emotional support";[3] they are also defined as places that facilitate "the regular, voluntary, informal, and happily anticipated gatherings of individuals beyond the realms of home and work."[4] Ray Oldenburg in his classic book, *The Great Good Place,* perhaps offers the best insight into these Third Places. Featuring several case studies, Oldenburg gives insight into such places that offer a friendly, welcoming place away from our homes (i.e., first places) and places of work (i.e., second places). Most of us might simply refer to such places with the qualifier "local": the local pub, local café, etc. Perhaps we all grew up knowing the proprietors who ran our local "places." Perhaps when we return to familiar cities or neighborhoods, we are keen to find out if our favorite Third Place is still there.

Of course, place is one thing, but it is the people within them that transform "places" into Third Places. Not all coffee shops or bars provide a home away from home, a place where our stories are shared or known, where we can feel comfortable slowly revealing

---

3. Saey and Foss, "The Third Place Experience," 1.
4. Oldenburg, *The Great Good Place,* 16.

Whatever Happened to the Rich Young Man?

more of our private selves. With the advent of many franchised coffee houses and pub chains, it (sadly) does not follow that the social experience within them matches the local Third Places we may have known and loved growing up. Jerry Mander sums up the situation well:

> Place separated from the people who inhabit it becomes a mere fact, a calculation in a formula, subject to the application of power in the interest of profit. We pursue abstractions: removing what is personal and unique from the equation. What we fail to see is that when we franchise fast food, we abstract humanity itself.[5]

Basically, if we leave the "people" considerations and sense of well-being out of our franchised business model, then the danger is that the sense of community can be significantly impacted. The sad thing is, if sociologists are right, then as a human race, we have been volunteering to participate in this "individualism" project for many years.[6] Suffice to say, Robert Putnam captured this in his landmark article "Bowling Alone," which he later expanded into a book. Here, he draws a direct and causal connection between the increasing isolation and individualism in US society and the breakdown of communities.[7] Thus, beyond the obvious and measured needs of our local communities, there is another need that everyone is feeling the impact of.

The need for the reemergence of local Third Places, assisted with both theological and sociological insights, can help people discover what it means to be a community again. Yet not simply a community encouraged to "connect" again, but one that at the same time invites others into a welcoming Kingdom community of God's people.

---

5. Quoted in Hjalmarson, *No Place Like Home*, 27.

6. For a fuller treatment of this subject, see Hardy and Foster, *Body and Blood*, 1–7.

7. Putnam, *Bowling Alone*.

HOW MIGHT THE CHURCH RESPOND?

As churches accustomed to responding to local and measured need, the development of local Third Places that enhance local communities and offer an opportunity to encounter faith is something I was keen to research. Chapters 5 and 6 will present case studies of two such places endeavoring to do this. The disappearing "grazing land" of Third Places should be of serious interest to any church seeking to impact and engage with its community. It may be that this simply takes the form of frequenting the already existing local place. Many churches offer seeker courses, outreach and worship evenings in cafes. These are all well and good, but this approach misses the point, somewhat. It misunderstands the sociological importance and centrality of building (to use Oldenburg's terminology) "Great Good Places" that authenticate social connection, yet with a gospel intentionality. "Parachuting into" a local place and running the occasional course or evening is commendable and can provide a helpful platform upon which one can invite known, local, friendly contacts. However, the development of a trusted Third Place operating at the heart of its community and seen as a central "totem" of importance by the locals takes time. In the language of discipleship, if the infrequent worship evenings provide the "come and see" spaces where the crowds can safely come, observe, but not necessarily commit, then the local, friendly, and familiar Third Places provide the more intimate "come and follow" spaces where would-be disciples of Jesus can be called and shaped.

Of course, there are always testimonies of how "one-off" public events may have positively impacted an individual for Christ, with such events often being an encouraging catalyst for further discussion. Yet for ongoing, long-term impact, local Third Places run by faith-based organizations provide a secure and familiar "fishing pond" for conversation and discussion, where day by day, week by week, local people can build trust, friendships, and an openness to Christ while at the same time seeing the witness and interactions of the community of God's people. So, the important factor to understand is that building Third Places takes *time*, investment in a specific place, and people. Whatever aspiring adjectives

Whatever Happened to the Rich Young Man?

we may allocate to a place or event (e.g., family, home, welcome, etc.), there is no substitute for invested time into local place and the people who frequent it. Oldenburg, in his follow-up book *Celebrating the Third Place*, warns against the creation of "counterfeit" Third Places, as opposed to what he describes as the "real thing":

> Developers build houses and call them "homes." They build socially sterile subdivisions and call them "communities." It's called "warming the product." It's also happening with alleged Third Places. Officials of a popular coffee house chain often claim that their establishments are Third Places, but they aren't. They may evolve into them, but at present, they are high-volume, fast-turnover operations that present an institutional ambience at an intimate level. Seating is uncomfortable by design and customers in line are treated rudely when uncertain of their orders.[8]

Oldenburg goes on to lament that while certain establishments may claim Third Place status, they ultimately do not deliver a true Third Place experience.[9]

Third Places are special. They provide an oasis of friendly conversation, genuine personal interest, and home-away-from-home surroundings that facilitate belonging and community. They are much needed in our communities and they are disappearing fast. As a gathering of God's people keen to meet the local needs of our communities (beyond welfare), the development of Third Places with the dual objective of enhancing a community's well-being with a gospel intentionality provides us with an incredible opportunity.

WHAT TYPE OF PLACE?

Building Third Places is one thing: developing them with such dual objectives is quite another. This needs careful and prayerful thought

---

8. Oldenburg, *Celebrating the Third Place*, 3.
9. Oldenburg, *Celebrating the Third Place*, 4.

Negotiating the Third Place

and planning. General, detailed, and more practical questions need to be asked:

a. What sort of Third Place do we envisage?
b. What would be a good location?
c. What sort of staff would be suitable?
d. How would we communicate within the staff team the dual objectives of community enhancement and gospel intentionality?
e. Would all staff need to buy into the dual vision?
f. What sort of costs are involved in keeping the Third Place open?
g. How would this fit with the demographic of our local community?

All of these questions (and more) are essential prerequisites for any church or faith-based organization desiring to embark on such a Third-Place venture. There is a great need for churches to be able to "read" their local communities. A poorly planned project, however well-meaning, can do more damage than good to a church's or organization's reputation. Reading the local community involves paying attention to local people, their stories, and their folklore. It means knowing the local buildings, their history, and their importance. A ministry colleague of mine wanted to start a community center as the basis for a church plant on a run-down estate in Edinburgh. Wanting to communicate their community values to the locals, they decided to embark on a door-to-door program telling people about the new "community church." Responses were polite or indifferent. Then during one particular conversation, while describing the location of the new initiative, one middle-aged woman exclaimed, "Ah, you mean ye ol' mission hall! My nanny took us there wan we wo' kids!" Suddenly, the conversation turned from indifference and suspicion to shared stories of packed halls, music evenings, and the "good ol' days." From that point, the door-to-door team announced they were from the "ol' mission hall" and were seeking to recreate the lost community with a "twist" of faith. The difference in response was staggering. Reading our communities matters. Knowing our communities matters. If the recent

COVID-19 pandemic has highlighted anything, it has been people's openness to "community," to appreciating that we need each other. Well-planned Third Places facilitate this well. Yet in addition to practically planning and knowing the required approach, it is equally important that *theologically* our understanding is clear, too. This theology is summarized in three words: Place, Kingdom, and Gospel.

A THEOLOGY OF PLACE

God loves place. God incarnates, gets in the mix of, gets messy in place. From the very beginning, God in all his creative glory created a place for mankind to inhabit, preparing the environment first and then mankind as his creative pinnacle. Ever since that moment, following our catastrophic "fall" from our privileged, created position, God has set in motion his redemptive plan to restore mankind and his creation back to himself in the context of "place." God said to Abraham:

> Go from your country, your people and your father's household to the land I will show you. I will make you into a great nation, and I will bless you; I will make your name great, and you will be a blessing. I will bless those who bless you, and whoever curses you I will curse; and all peoples on earth will be blessed through you. (Gen 12:1–3)

This restoration was ultimately realized and executed at Calvary, the place of the cross, and will finally be consummated in a new "place," described in the book of Revelation:

> Then I saw "a new heaven and a new earth," for the first heaven and the first earth had passed away, and there was no longer any sea. I saw the Holy City, the new Jerusalem, coming down out of heaven from God, prepared as a bride beautifully dressed for her husband. And I heard a loud voice from the throne saying, "Look! God's dwelling place is now among the people, and he will dwell with them. They will be his people, and God himself will

be with them and be their God. He will wipe every tear from their eyes. There will be no more death or mourning or crying or pain, for the old order of things has passed away." (Rev 21:1–4)

This wonderful culmination and summary of God's completed restorative work happens and results in "place." God in place creates something new, beautiful, restorative, comforting; but above all he creates a place where he is in the center. Third Places seek to emulate this theology by creating places at the heart of our communities that restore, beautify, and center around the God who made and loved us.

Yet central to such a strategy is the development of an approach that seeks to *incarnate,* to dwell amongst, be in the midst of. The Message version of John's Gospel translates this well as it explains Christ's approach to our messy, fallen world:

> The Word became flesh and blood, and moved into the neighborhood. We saw the glory with our own eyes, the one-of-a-kind glory, like Father, like Son, Generous inside and out, true from start to finish. (John 1:14 MSG)

As Christ's ambassadors, our approach to community is to emulate the one we represent. Like him, we move into our neighborhoods and are generous inside and out and true to our Master's commission. Place is to be central to our theology and approach.

A KINGDOM THEOLOGY

What is to be our mandate and manifesto by which we conduct ourselves once in that "place"? Developing a *Kingdom* mindset as ambassadors of the one we represent is to be central to our approach. Early in his ministry, when sending out the seventy-two, Luke tells us that Jesus sent his disciples out ahead of him to various places, instructing them to declare his Kingdom *peace* [*shalom*], to eat and drink whatever was put in front of them, and to declare the *Kingdom* [*basileia*] of God was near (Luke 10:5–10). Prior to the cross (Jesus was still alive!), prior to justification by faith, and

Whatever Happened to the Rich Young Man?

underpinning all of our practiced and rehearsed orthodoxies (right teaching), God's people are to represent King Jesus in local places and declare his *shalom*-rule, one that crosses all cultural and social barriers, that the King may come in. A Kingdom (or Jesus rule) mindset prepares a platform for him. Our Third Places are to be places that announce the good news of the Kingdom, but equally as important, the good news of the cross. Thus there is a need for places that enhance community, yet do so with a gospel intentionality.

A GOSPEL DISTINCTIVE

Understanding the importance of a theology of place while underpinning this with a Kingdom theology is critical, yet where many well-meaning projects fail is in our third word, Gospel. There are plenty of good and kind groups doing lots of good and kind things within their communities. People from other faiths, people of no faith, charity groups, scout groups, all with the honorable desire to serve and "give back" are involved at the heart of our communities. However, God's approach to mission always has a purpose, a *gospel* purpose. Very early on in his ministry, Jesus would refer to his ultimate purpose to, "suffer many things" (Mark 8:31). Within that same chapter of Mark's Gospel, Jesus would announce, "For even the Son of Man did not come to be served, but to serve, and give his life as a ransom for many" (Mark 8:45). As unpopular as Jesus' statements were to both his disciples and his enemies, equally today God's people can recoil from declaring the good news of the life, death, resurrection, and return of King Jesus. Tim Chester cautions against such an exclusion, ultimately describing "gospel-less" projects as, "signposts pointing nowhere."[10]

THEOLOGY AND SOCIOLOGY: AN UNLIKELY PARTNERSHIP

One thing I have learned over the course of my doctoral research is the importance of coming out from my theological enclave. By

---

10. Chester, *Good News to the Poor*, 65.

this, I mean emerging out of the safe world of theology, church-based meetings and projects and gatherings, and "mixing it up" a little with (what is often referred to as) the secular academy. My interactions with sociologists, many of whom possess a "gospel-less" interest in the development of Third Places, has encouraged me to seek the best of both disciplines. This can (and must) work both ways. In addition to the social sciences informing our theology, there is an informing role for theology, too. Since our communities are comprised of many varied people groups, many of whom will possess some sort of God-based (theistic) view of life (worldview), both academic voices need to be heard.

Having said all that, I want to keep this book practical. So, bringing together these two disciplines (theology and sociology), how might they inform a Third-Place project, out of a faith-based organization, that possesses the joint objectives of enhancing a community and sharing the gospel intentionally? The next three chapters will demonstrate this as we start to look into the faith-based Third Places I investigated—cafés.

Chapter 4

Café Ethnography: A Unique Opportunity

SO WHAT'S SO SPECIAL ABOUT CAFÉS?

Not all cafés are Third Places and not all Third Places are cafés; yet there is something about the café/coffee shop[1] that is broadly appealing to most people. Perhaps meeting up with a special friend, having that special treat. Even those who do not particularly like coffee will usually find something in a café that they enjoy, such as hot chocolate, a milkshake, or one of those specialty cakes! In broad terms, we probably envisage the café to be a place that ranges from the local, friendly, "all-day breakfast" establishment to the more upmarket "panini and latte" house. Moreover, the "coffee house" can be defined by its name (i.e., a "house of coffee") specializing in a (perhaps) previously unknown range of international and artisan coffees. Either way, both have the potential to acquire Third Place status within the communities in which they are located. But this status is not automatic, as some have assumed. As mentioned in the previous chapter, developing local Third Places that become part of our community folklore, and that are seen as totems of identity

---

1. I use these interchangeably, although some coffee connoisseurs would challenge this!

and hubs of community, friendship, and belonging, takes time and intentionality.

Yet what about the *physical* aspects of such Third Places? Sociologists (for many years) have been researching this whole area of what is referred to as *café ethnography*. Sociologists give their attention not only to the *people* aspects but also to the "product" (what is sold), as well as other aspects such as place and machinery. How do such aspects as lighting, café layout, type of coffee-producing machinery, impact any Third Place "signature"? This chapter will give an insight into some of these important aspects, asking how they (along with the importance of having the right people) might play their part in creating a Third Place conducive to conversation, friendship, and a general sense of belonging.

To facilitate this, it might be helpful if I tell you a little story. I am certain we have all been to "those" places—places where our experience has been less than satisfactory or affirming. I can recall one such time when I was in-between appointments and found myself near a coffee house that I had previously never visited. I had thirty minutes or so prior to my next meeting and had arrived in the area early—an ideal time for a quick break and maybe a small treat! Generally being quite cheerful, I like to think that I am fairly easy to chat with. I entered the coffee house and there was nobody in the queue. Great! Two baristas stood behind the counter, their backs to me—talking with each other when not checking their cellphones. In what seemed like an age, I stood there, read the menu (knowing I wanted a hot chocolate!), and fiddled with my credit card. Eventually, one of the baristas turned around, finished her text, looked up, and asked what I would like. No apology or cheerful greeting. In fact, I felt that I had interrupted her conversation and "text-thought flow." I was an inconvenience. I ordered my hot chocolate, paid, then waited at the counter (since I wasn't sure where I was supposed to wait), as the barista (again) had her back to me as she prepared the drink. Of course, *that* wasn't her fault. The positioning of the equipment that discouraged barista/patron interaction further impacted my experience. The barista passed me the drink and said nothing. Eye contact was reserved for her phone. I thanked her (my parents taught me well!) and went to look for a seat. It wasn't that there weren't any seats, but the first two tables I saw were uncleared. I was getting the strong impression that the baristas were finding the details of their work a great distraction to their social media status! I drank my hot chocolate and left for my meeting.

Within that single account, you may have discerned some of the essential aspects of café ethnography that sociologists, and specifically those who research Third Places, are fascinated by. These sociological aspects are critical to keep in mind as we seek to develop Third Places conducive to discussion, friendship, and belonging. I have summarized these collective aspects of Third Places under the headers *people, product, place, and machinery,* to which we will now turn.

PEOPLE

Having the right people as we seek to develop a Third Place is paramount. One can have the best equipment, trendiest lighting, and widest offering of products, but it is the *people* that will transform a community or high-street establishment (whether it be a franchised chain or not) into a loved and local Third Place that encourages interaction between staff, volunteers, and patrons. Now it may be part of the strategy of a Third Place run by a faith-based organization to include within their staff teams those who do not (as yet) profess any faith in Christ. This approach might come under what some have referred to as a "belonging before you believe" approach. This can work with great discernment, as long as the associated risks have been considered. What might these be? In my experience, things can start well when there is a higher ratio of Christ-followers to those who are (as yet) not. However, often with the best intentions, all too often I have seen such ratios even out, or even swing the other way. This is not a unique issue with Third Places. This can happen with any faith-based project or ministry, be it a football team, craft club, youth club, or other. The issue may not seem obvious. It might even appear a little paranoid. Yet the important thing to understand is that *every* person who serves within any project or ministry adds their own "signature." We all have a "worldview":

Café Ethnography: A Unique Opportunity

ideas about life, death, faith, heaven, hell, and eternity. We all possess opinions about sexuality, marriage, and what matters in life in general. Every person contributes to this signature—collectively impacting the overall "team signature"—including any values communicated. The challenge here is that, in the eyes of the patrons, everyone they engage with in that Third Place represents the organization behind it. The views and attitudes they see on display, if misrepresentative of Christ, will at best (potentially) damage the reputation of the church or organization involved; at worst, it will misrepresent the King and his Kingdom, the one whom the whole project is desiring to represent and communicate. I am not saying that "belonging before you believe" is not a good strategy, or that it should not form part of the overall approach. I am simply cautioning against its overuse. Awareness of the dangers can be helpful.

Equally, it does not follow that recruiting staff or volunteers who are professing Christ-followers will be any better. We are all works in progress. Like any other ministry setting, a faith-based Third Place is a calling. Interviewing prospective staff is important. Do they understand and support the vision of the café? Do they have a personal "Christ-following" story to tell? Do they model what it means to follow King Jesus? Do they feel a sense of calling to the work? Do they have a servant heart? Do they have a heart for people? If the answer to these questions is yes, then your team will be in good shape to serve as Christ's ambassadors. Having the right people can cover a multitude of early mishaps as the team and the café are brought up to speed to be the best they can be for him.

Having great people working in our Third Places is central to their success. This said, we must not underestimate the importance of the physical aspects, either. Patrons who are already known to the staff or volunteers, who may come in for a friendly chat, may well forgive a sub-par experience. In churches, we tend to put up with the average (if well-meaning) offering of instant coffee or weak tea. We think, "This is family, after all." Yet, Third Place reputations can easily be lost in the details of other important aspects such as product, place, and machinery. I will now deal with each of these (non-human) aspects in turn, with the hope that this will give helpful insight into the role each of these play in the creation of a Third Place.

PRODUCT

So, having spoken about the *people* side of things, what about the *product?* I have mentioned that within our churches we can generally get away with less-than-average refreshments. After all, it is the *people* we are there for. Yet as we move out into the public sphere, we are entering a whole new world of challenge. When people pay for goods and services, they have different expectations. That coffee that tastes like tea won't do. Although the franchised chains can be socially sterile and impersonal, they generally know how to make good coffee. When I pastored a church in the West Midlands (UK), we opened a local café. One of the first decisions we made was to purchase a proper coffee machine, then bring in a barista trainer to train our volunteer team. Caring about the quality of our product can help us communicate that we care for the people, too. Many other things matter, often small things, such as having napkins available, displaying our food in an attractive way, and clearing tables in a timely manner (though not too keen!). I will say more about this when I write about the details of the place; suffice to say, these things matter. Just think of any complaint or concern you may have had when you visited a similar establishment: cold food (that should be hot), stale cakes, lukewarm drinks, dirty cups, and so on. Once we go public, these things really matter.

PLACE

People and products are essential factors in a café if it is to develop into a Third Place. Patrons will come back for friendly conversations and good food and refreshments. Additionally, news about being a friendly environment with high-quality products will travel fast. This said, paying attention to what sort of physical place we create really matters. If we each think about our own experiences, the overall comfort, layout, and general ambiance assist greatly in providing the sort of environment where meaningful Third Places conversations can be cultivated and encouraged. Lisa Waxman conducted research into a number of coffee shops. She focused on ascertaining the top *physical* (non-human) elements that patrons considered to be important.[2] Summarizing her research, Waxman states:

> The key findings regarding the physical characteristics showed the top five design considerations included: cleanliness, appealing aroma, adequate lighting, comfortable furniture, and a view to the outside. A number of themes emerged related to people, their activities, and their feelings and attitudes regarding the coffee shop. Each coffee shop was found to have a unique social climate and culture related to a sense of belonging, territoriality, ownership, productivity, and personal growth, opportunity for socialization, support and networking, and sense of community. Regarding feelings of community, survey findings from coffee shops patrons showed a positive correlation between length of patronage and their sense of attachment to their community.[3]

The above physical factors that contribute to the overall perception of Third Places such as cafés can be summarized under the theory of *place attachment*. As a comparison, people who work with "looked-after children"[4] know the importance of attachment theory with regards its impact on a child's social and integrative skills. Regarding Third Places, place attachment is also a critical theory for consideration. Again, Waxman informs us:

> The experience of place is unique to each individual and is directly related to his or her lived experiences. Attachment to place is a set of feelings that emotionally binds people to a particular place.[5]

2. Waxman, "The Coffee Shop."
3. Waxman, "The Coffee Shop," 35.
4. This term is used within the UK social services to refer to any child within the care system who are cared for outside of their normal parental home/environment.
5. Waxman, "The Coffee Shop," 36.

Whatever Happened to the Rich Young Man?

Our own experiences of place attachment bear this out. Both good and bad places hold memories and provide visible milestones of our life's experiences: The feeling you have when you drive past your old school, that old factory or office block where you used to work, the local landmark that hails your arrival home, and those Third Places where conversations, acceptance, and community were nurtured. Places embed themselves within our psyches. Keeping this in mind when developing our very own Third Places can encourage us to ask ourselves some important questions: What sort of memories will this place evoke in people? How might this place become a place of acceptance, friendship, and mutual understanding?

MACHINERY

The thought of machines impacting our social interaction may (at first) appear to be somewhat extreme, perhaps even evoking thoughts from the latest sci-fi thriller! While it may not be as dramatic as that when it comes to the impact of machinery on Third Places, it is important enough to attract the attention of sociologists and café ethnographers. John Manzo is one such researcher. He produced a 2014 paper entitled, "Machines, People, and Social Interaction in 'Third-Wave' Coffeehouses."[6] Manzo's use of the term "Third Wave" is not to be confused with "Third Place." Third wave in this context speaks about (what Manzo terms) "high-end" coffee-producing equipment—those "houses of coffee" I mentioned in our earlier definitions. In his paper, Manzo compares the coffee-producing machinery of a number of coffee houses and importantly how this machinery contributes to staff/patron interaction. For Manzo:

> Humans interact not only with one another, but also with, and conditioned through, the natural and built environment in which sociality takes place, and the objects that those environments comprise.

6. Manzo, "'Third-Wave' Coffeehouses."

My earlier story at the beginning of this chapter outlined one of the impacts of poorly-positioned machinery (remember, it positioned the barista's back to me?). Everything within our Third Places matters and contributes to the overall ambiance, sense of welcome, and comfort, which all give rise to meaningful conversations.

MARS HILL CAFÉ: CREATING THE PLACE FOR DISCUSSION

Developing a Third-Place café to encourage a sense of community and facilitate "talk about Jesus" is an exciting challenge, one that needs the insights from both theology and sociology. While our theology will inform our motivations (with the desire to see lives transformed for Christ), sociology will inform our practical approach. We have already seen the importance of people, products, place, and machinery. There are many other "people and place" factors that we need to be aware of that will collectively assist our Third-Place objectives. Sociologically, some are simple but still important—such as magazines and reading materials that encourage patrons to linger, loyalty cards that reward regular use, community "buy one forward" schemes that allow patrons to buy an extra coffee for someone else, and free internet to encourage work, study, and other online activities. This said, the jury is out with regard to whether or not, when it comes to the creation of a Third Place, free internet is a good thing or not. All too often, cafés can inadvertently become "study hubs" with tables full of isolated patrons locked into their own focused world. The sounds and ambiance of the Third Place is blocked out by headphones. If creating a Third Place conducive to meaningful conversation is the central objective, perhaps the potential impact of internet needs to be an early conversation.

Yet there are theological lessons that can be learned too when it comes to our approach to the development of a Third Place. Some of these lessons can be learned from the approach of the Apostle Paul during his second missionary journey in Acts 17. Within that chapter, Luke gives us the account of Paul in Athens (Acts 17:16–34). As well as the synagogue, the writer tells us that Paul finds himself in the marketplace, the local "talk shop," where "All the Athenians and the foreigners who lived there spent their time doing nothing but talking about and listening to the latest ideas" (Acts 17:21). In the midst of this, Paul was given the opportunity to share about faith, life, death, resurrection, and judgment. Yet prior to this, Paul had familiarized himself with the local icons, customs, and folklore. He was even able to quote some of the people's own poets within the context of his message (Acts 17:28). Within a familiar marketplace context, known locally by the Greeks as the Areopagus (or Mars Hill to the Romans), Paul was able to communicate his faith and hope in the resurrected Christ.

As we build our Third Places within our local "marketplaces" (or communities of discussion), it is essential that we familiarize ourselves with the local folklore, customs, and worldviews. As both the UK and the US become more post-Christian, we can no longer assume that people will be familiar with the founding narratives of our faith. Just like Mars Hill, our Third-Place cafés can become places of faith-based conversation, yet equally, we need to be mindful of the aforementioned sociological aspects of Third Place, too—factors that will provide an important platform that facilitate open discussion and friendship.

So, having said all this, does it actually work? Is it possible to develop a Third Place with the dual aim of enhancing local community yet doing so with a gospel intentionality? There are plenty of "how-to" books on the shelves that encourage the church to venture out into projects that in concept sound great, but are there any actual examples? I did not want to simply write another "how-to" book with a clever theory and one or two anecdotal stories. Thus, for the past two years I have been researching two cafés that have been endeavouring to do just that, create Third Places to enhance their local communities and provide platforms for gospel conversations. The next two chapters will give some insights into my research, with names of cafés, churches, patrons, and more, all changed in the name of research ethics. We shall call these cafés the Welcome Café and the Friendship Café.

Chapter 5

A Tale of Two Cafés, Part 1: The Friendship Café

It has been my privilege over the past two years to be allowed free and open access to two West Midlands cafés, both run by faith-based organizations. Although both organizations were out of different church affiliations, both considered themselves to be *evangelical* in the sense of subscribing to the four classic tenets of evangelicalism outlined by David Bebbington: activism, biblicism, crucicentrism, and conversionism.[1] In my early interviews with the leadership and management of both cafés, they each expressed their objective was to create a café that enhanced the sense of local community, but doing so with a desire to see lives transformed for Christ with a gospel intentionality. This was (what some would call) their *espoused* position, what they *said* their objectives were. Both cafés also acknowledged their desire to reach a broad demographic of people, including (what I have termed) the New Marginalized. The subsequent two years of research, which involved many hours sitting in both cafés (some research can be fun!) provided rich

1. Bebbington, *Evangelicalism in Modern Britain*. Activism refers to the need for faith to be seen in action; biblicism, the position that the bible informs all of life; crucicentrism, the centrality of the Christ and the cross; conversionism, the need for lives to be transformed for Christ.

and helpful insights into how successful (or not!) the cafés were at achieving these objectives. I am grateful to the management and staff of both cafés for allowing me to ask awkward questions and see these "works in progress." I have divided my considerations and findings of each café into two chapters (part one and part two.) Following a little research background, these chapters will give some (hopefully helpful) insights into what I found as I strived to find out whatever happened to the rich young man. Perhaps he was alive and well and sitting at one of the tables, waiting for a second chance.

RESEARCH BACKGROUND

As I mentioned in the introduction to this book, I have always had an interest, since my very own days in industry (particularly senior management), in the church's relationship with the New Marginalized, those who are identified as self-sufficient and without any obvious or presenting needs. I had consistently felt this disconnect between my corporate life and my church life. I think I always endeavored to represent Christ well in the various corporate roles in which I found myself, but I could not see any obvious connection or church program I could invite my corporate friends and colleagues into. As an evangelist at heart, I was happy to be "in the mix," sharing Jesus when opportunity arose, but I still had this nagging question: "How can the church engage with this (apparently) self-sufficient demographic?"

The issue was never really resolved, and even when I entered full-time ministry, the gap seemed even wider from inside the church's perspective. At least prior to ministry, I was able to incarnate and get in the mix of all things corporate. Thus, when the opportunity arose to embark on a course of doctoral study, I wondered if this might be the opportunity I had been waiting for. Yet doctoral research has to contribute new insights in two key areas: practice and theory. What new theories would any such research contribute? And what new practical insights would this reveal and encourage? My first two years of study at Roehampton University were designed to primarily find out what the "gaps" in practice and theory were in this field. Perhaps others had already researched and covered this. I summarized my approach to this in chapter two, outlining how through conversations and discussions with Professors Paul Cloke and Chris Baker, I was able to position my research accordingly, as a new contribution. Somehow, I was not surprised when I discovered that very little had been written about reaching the self-sufficient demographic with the gospel. One helpful book I did find was one written by Bishop Richard Harries (previous Bishop of Oxford), entitled, *Is there a Gospel for the Rich?*[2] Yet this was a non-research-based if well-written piece of work. Following discussions with my doctoral supervisors, it was becoming clear that my proposed research was indeed new ground.

Having narrowed down the focus of my research to investigate how evangelical Third Places might facilitate gospel conversations with the New Marginalized, I then proceeded to identify potential research locations. Two such cafés, out of evangelical traditions, became the focus. While they would not articulate their mission in the language of an academic thesis or research program, both had expressed their desire to create a place that contributed to the local sense of community, but do so with a desire to share Jesus. These two Third Places we shall call the Friendship Café and the Welcome Café. Let's look at each café in turn and seek to capture something of what I found during my time in each.

THE FRIENDSHIP CAFÉ

Situated in Coventry, the Friendship Café is part of the outreach strategy of Phoenix Church,[3] a medium-sized independent evangelical church. Phoenix Church had itself been through a significant paradigm shift with regard to its own identity and strategy prior to opening the café in the summer of 2016. From 2009 to 2016, the church had been involved in developing a *missional* approach to reaching the surrounding area of its church. Prior to this, the church's general approach was *attractional,* basically putting

---

2. Harries, *Is there a Gospel for the Rich?*
3. Names of places and persons have been changed for confidentiality.

on various events within the confines of its building, then inviting people to attend. This missional paradigm shift resulted in a number of what may be called *incarnational* projects (community based as opposed to church based), including allotments, music projects, plus the Friendship Café. Prior to Phoenix Church opening the café in 2016, the café unit had been leased from the local council by another nearby city church for a number of years. Just prior to 2016, the facility had largely fell into disuse, though still offering an early morning breakfast club for the local school and a youth club for local teenagers one evening per week. The leadership of Phoenix Church, with a new missional vision, saw this as an opportunity to position themselves within the heart of the community while at the same time revitalizing the project. Thus, they approached the leadership of their neighboring church to discuss the possibility of developing a café as a joint project. This was received warmly, with a joint café being set up and launched in June 2016. A year later, Phoenix Church took on the sole running of the café as their partner church moved their vision and focus into a different part of the city.

The Friendship Café needed a significant amount of work to bring it up to the standards of a public café. In addition to meeting public and legislative expectations of a community café, the management were also keen to have a clear vision. This vision could be summarized with two overall objectives: to provide a café that enhanced the local sense of community, and to provide a place that facilitated gospel conversations with a broad demographic of people. Practical aspects of the café also had to be considered: What will be the menu range? What price levels should we set? What hours should we (and can we) open? Who will join the café team? What sort of skills and people do we need? In order to fulfil the dual vision of the café, the management agreed that they would need to divide staff between those who could cover the practical tasks (cooking, serving, stock check, etc.), and those who would be gifted at sharing life and faith stories with any patrons who would frequent the café.

A Tale of Two Cafés, Part 1: The Friendship Café

THE EARLY MONTHS

I mentioned earlier that the language of Third Place and New Marginalized would not be necessarily used by the café management and volunteers to describe what they were doing. This is often the case; theory can be a helpful tool, but we must not leave out the inspiration of the Holy Spirit. Much of our systematic theology and theories are worked out in retrospect as we reflect on the activity of God. Theories and academia can go only so far when it comes to informing our projects. This said, it was interesting to interpret the development of (and interactions within) the café in the light of this theory. In the previous two chapters, I summarized the aspects of Third Place and café ethnography in both theological and sociological terms. In chapter three, I spoke about the theological categories of place, Kingdom, and gospel. In chapter four, our considerations in café ethnography were categorized into people, product, place, and machinery. For the remainder of this chapter, I will deal with these theological and sociological aspects, beginning with the latter.

THE PEOPLE OF THE FRIENDSHIP CAFÉ

This, for me, is always the most interesting part: seeing the interactions of the people groups. Of course, this could be considered under two broad categories: interactions within the staff team, and interactions between the staff and patrons of the café. After all, it would be these interactions that would provide the core of the research outcomes. I had so many questions to find answers to:

a. What was the understanding of each staff member within the café, with regard to their purposes and objectives?
b. Was this espoused understanding reflected in what they said and did in the café?
c. What was the patrons opinions of the café, with regard to its impact on the local sense of community?
d. Had the patrons experienced any faith-based conversations and how did they feel about this?

e. What did the patrons feel about the dual objectives of the café team?

Before I outline my findings and answers to these questions, it would be useful to introduce the staff and patrons of the Friendship Café to you.

THE TEAM

Lesley was the one to whom the Lord gave the original vision. A member of Phoenix Church's leadership team, Lesley had always had a passion to serve Jesus. It was Lesley's passion that the former tenants of the café saw in the presentation, and it was this that gave them the confidence to approve the original joint-working proposal. Lesley was great with people, great at making cakes, and she communicated the love and compassion of Jesus to those around her. Lesley had recently graduated with a first-class theology degree from a West Midlands Bible College. She majored in missional theology, which encouraged an incarnational and imaginative approach to mission. This collective background had ideally prepared Lesley to lead and manage the café project.

Yet as willing and able as Lesley was, good leaders realize that ministry thrives as we build successful teams that collectively understand and share the same vision. Phoenix Church was blessed by having its own training academy, part of which was connected to that same West Midland Bible College. A number of the students were placed at the church as part of their degree course; thus, this supplied a group of people, all of whom were embarking upon a missional course of study, to volunteer and serve at the café. Enhancing this were a number of local people: a young family who had come to Christ in recent years and had started attending the church (Mike and Stacey), plus Dave, a local guy who had an interest in matters of faith, but predominantly wanted to "play his part" in the local community. Other members of Phoenix Church would help out, too—including the pastor and associate pastor. Thus, the vast majority of the team were members of Phoenix Church, all understood the vision and values of the church, and all were

A Tale of Two Cafés, Part 1: The Friendship Café

passionate about making Jesus known. A further significant factor in the team was that they were all volunteers. No paid staff. They served because they wanted to.

This all sounds pretty "textbook," but it was not without its issues. As people, we take ourselves with us everywhere we go. Please do not read the absence of major conflict narratives as a sign that every day was smooth sailing. The individuals and teams had their issues, both personal and within the serving team. But they were available and willing, and that is all that God asks us to be.

THE PATRONS

The vast majority of the patrons that used the café were from the local houses, flats, and apartments surrounding the row of shops in which the café was situated. Additionally, professional workers (teachers, social workers, mental health workers, housing officers, et al) also frequented the café. Prior to this, Phoenix Church had been separated from the local area by a busy city-center link road. This road was perceived by many in the church as a huge barrier to connecting with the local estate. So, when the opportunity came to run a café in the heart of the community (across the road), this was seen as a real, God given opportunity.

Situated opposite a school, the café also attracted quite a large group of local mums and their preschool children. It was an ideal place to sit and have a coffee—you could arrive a few minutes early before needing to collect the older school-aged children. This created an interesting and varied patron base. Of course, my research needed to identify the New Marginalized frequenting the café. Devising good initial quantitative questionnaires is an essential part of any evidence-based research, and it needs to be designed in such a way that the demographic of interest can be identified for further research, if necessary. Setting out the key parameters for one's research is an important prerequisite. Once my initial questionnaire had identified the right demographic, I was then keen to find out what they felt about the café in general, but more specifically how

Whatever Happened to the Rich Young Man?

they perceived the joint café objectives of enhancing the sense of local community and faith-sharing.

This all said, research can sound a little cold and statistical. Behind each interview, I was aware there was a person whom Jesus loved deeply. I was keen to hear their stories, get to know them better, and not to be obsessed with my own research agenda. I did not want to view them as targets of theological and sociological research, but objects of God's love. I found the research and subsequent ad hoc conversations fulfilling and personally enriching. These were real people behind the (assumed) self-sufficient display. There was Annabelle, the mental health professional whose daughter was in hospital with serious mental health issues manifested by an eating disorder; Ruth, the special-needs professional who would meet up in the café with her husband Mike three times a week; Mike was diagnosed with a personality disorder; Rami was a driving instructor who was trying to build up his business; there was Lucy, a local youth worker whose youth club was under threat of closure due to a lack of government funding. These are real people, real lives, all needing Jesus. I will bring out much of my conversations with these wonderful people in the sections below, but I never wanted to lose sight of the human story contained in each one. The rich young man still had questions he needed answers to.

THE PRODUCTS OF THE FRIENDSHIP CAFÉ

We mentioned earlier that great products can enhance a Third-Place experience. In a public café, people want good food at a good value. By and large, the Friendship Café delivered on both. Every café and eatery has its mishaps, so I certainly witnessed the occasional overly frothed latte and dubious-looking fried egg! However, this was the exception rather than the rule. Additionally, the café had a "no quibble" replacement policy: if you were not fully satisfied, they were happy to replace or refund your order. Having said this, one important factor that I sensed impacted the patron's view of the presented products was the fact that none of the team were paid professionals. Word got around that the running of the café was subsidized by the church's own training academy. This was reflected in the very reasonably priced menu. A major aspect of the café that ingratiated the patrons even further was the "buy one forward" scheme, where patrons could pay for an "extra" coffee, cake, or breakfast, which subsequently, as needs were identified, would be given free of charge to a grateful recipient. The coffee was "real" coffee. Hilariously, Lesley, the café's manager, really did not like the smell of coffee! Clearly, the Lord has a sense of humor. Lesley's freshly baked cakes were also a real hit with the patrons. Overall, on people and products, the Friendship Café scored high marks. A few patron quotes from my face to face, semi-structured interviews might help:

> I do recommend people to come over, especially in my little office . . . you just can't beat the friendliness and the food's lovely . . . you feel like you're putting something back into the community by coming here. (Joselin, support worker, young adult project)

> This café for me did not seem like a usual café. It was not business-focused: it was community- and people-minded. People took real intention in knowing names and just generally showing an interest where people were in their lives, and I felt it was a very wonderful experience that I took back with me to my office. When I shared it with colleagues, it made quite an impression. (Lucy, youth worker)

Even within these two general quotes from patrons, we can see the impression that the café was having. Both the people and the product were key in the creation of such an impression. Both people and product would contribute to the sociological sense of place attachment we mentioned in chapter 4; however, there are other important factors that also have a contribution to make, to which we shall now turn.

Whatever Happened to the Rich Young Man?

THE FRIENDSHIP CAFÉ AS SOCIOLOGICAL PLACE

Our attachment to place is formed by memorable encounters. Some of these encounters might be over a long period of time, perhaps as friendships are formed. These can take place in workplaces, places of education, places we lived, as well as Third Places—those places that provided a home away from home. Of course, place attachment can come out of a whole array of experiences. The Third-Place encounter is just one, but perhaps other experiences can forge place memories, too. Family homes of past abuses can impact our place perception; a workplace where we were bullied can also taint our view of certain places. For the purposes of this section, we are speaking about those *positive* Third-Place experiences that evoke warm, lasting memories and associations of belonging and friendship.

In chapter 4, I summarized Lisa Waxman's research into the five key physical factors that she found contributed most to place attachment: cleanliness, appealing aroma, adequate lighting, comfortable furniture, and a view to the outside. As I frequented both cafés, it was interesting to observe, not only my own sense of how these contributed to the sense of a Third Place, but also to hear from interviews with patrons the part these aspects played, too. With regard to cleanliness within food-producing establishments, one of the national (UK) measures is the Food Hygiene Rating. This is awarded by local authorities following an inspection. It scales from one to five stars. The Friendship Café proudly boasted its five-star rating on its main window display. Additionally, toward the end of each day, volunteers could be seen starting to sweep and mop the floors and the toilets were always well-stocked with an "inspection and cleaning" chart on the wall. Tables were kept clean. The light fittings were modern and clean and extra wall lights could be used to alter the atmosphere. Comfy sofas were arranged in one corner for both patrons and volunteers to sit and chat. A small children's play area with toys and books was designed to keep the children occupied. A bookshelf containing a range of magazines and books, including coloring books and (even) Bibles and children's Bible story books, encouraged patrons to stay and relax and gave an overall sense of welcome. The mixed aroma of freshly made

A Tale of Two Cafés, Part 1: The Friendship Café

coffee and "all-day breakfast" added to the atmosphere. The main entrance door was sandwiched between two large window displays, giving easy viewing to the passing world and of course an easy view into the café, too. With friendly, approachable staff, good food, a five-star hygiene rating and a high score on Waxman's non-human elements, this was shaping up (to use Oldenburg's earlier phrase) to be a "Great Good Place."

THE MACHINERY OF THE FRIENDSHIP CAFÉ

In chapter 4, I also made mention of Manzo's insights into the role of coffee-producing machinery in the creation of Third Places. This may seem a little bizarre to some, but referring back to my little story within that same chapter, machinery in the "wrong place" inadvertently plays its part, too. For the Friendship Café, this was not a major issue. The main machine was (in the artisan coffee world) a low-production machine designed for low-demand outlets. While the barista would still have to turn their back and focus on the machine while preparing the drinks, the process of ordering and the slow-to-steady influx of patrons meant conversations were not prejudiced by this, as they would often continue as a barista served patrons once the drink had been prepared. The position of the machine meant that it was unobtrusive, yet could still add to the sights, sounds, and aromas of the café.

To some extent, I hope highlighting these sociological factors has given important insight to those who would seek to develop such a Third Place, specifically one conducive to faith-based conversations. Maximizing these Third-Place factors creates an important platform upon which any spiritual objectives can be built. A simple exercise might be to imagine the opposite sociological experiences to the ones I have just described. Perhaps unfriendly staff, consistently poor food or drinks, dirty premises, poor lighting, a claustrophobic space, machinery that constantly and noisily demands attention and interrupts the overall ambience and capacity for staff and patrons to interact—these sociological factors helpfully inform and contribute to any would-be Third Place. During my interviews with the Friendship Café patrons, place-related comments frequently came out:

> People who come in here . . . feel safe to sit and talk and relax. (Annabelle)
>
> I think it's very welcoming, there's no loud music . . . it is about people. There are no hidden booths or its not in darkness, it's very open and very clear . . . the tables are nice and clean. (Lucy)
>
> I like the fact that it's small. It's always a friendly, relaxed atmosphere. It's a place you can go, even if you don't feel quite on top of things. . .the atmosphere makes you feel at ease. (Mike)

Collectively, these aspects can create a Third Place which by its very nature contributes to the local sense of community. While this is an honorable and important thing, especially as Third Places are disappearing from our community landscapes, the second objective of the Friendship Café was not only to develop such a community-enhancing place, but to do so with the intent to share Christ. I summarized these in chapter 3 with the concepts *Place, Kingdom,* and *Gospel*—theological aspects to which we shall now turn.

THE FRIENDSHIP CAFÉ AS THEOLOGICAL PLACE

Although we have made a distinction between sociological place and theological place, there is no such distinction in reality. Everywhere is God's place. The psalmist reminds us, "The earth is the Lord's, and everything in it, the world and all who live in it" (Ps 24:1). This all said, over the years (since the early-fourth century, to be precise), people (in and outside of the church) have tried to make a distinction between *sacred* and *secular* space. For those interested in studying this development further, James Thwaites gives this a good treatment in his book, *The Church Beyond the Congregation*.[4] In general, churches can feel more comfortable engaging

---

4. Thwaites, *The Church Beyond the Congregation*. Thwaites challenges the church to come out from what he describes as its "walled garden" and incarnate into the collective, wider spaces and places.

the not-yet-believers in their own "sacred" places. Perhaps there is a greater sense of permission and freedom to communicate their identity within the security of their own four walls. This is all well and good, and with regard to the development of a Third Place, can still be effective. However, local suspicions around religious organizations and motives may mean that people are less likely to invest in a church-based project. This will depend greatly on the existing reputation of the church in the community. In such cases, engaging with community gatekeepers would be essential in order to rebuild voices of trust in the community.

The Friendship Café had no such barriers. For the most part, new patrons were unaware (immediately) of the link with the local church. The café team had decided to restrict the use of overt, evangelical icons or displays. This was limited to a solitary picture with a single verse of scripture behind the counter. Additionally, the bookshelf had a range of regular books, but included some Bibles, children's Bible stories, and Christian biographies. So what was the main approach of the café team in seeking to create a place where God's presence could be felt and tangibly seen? The answer: the café team themselves were to be (as Paul could say to the Corinthian church) living letters: "For you yourselves are our letter, written on our hearts, known and read by everyone" (2 Cor 3:2). The team's openness to chat, pray, and share their faith journeys was the central strategy. Newbigin's living *hermeneutic of the gospel*. The relatively small size of the café, with six tables and a capacity to seat some twenty-five people at any one time, could make every conversation a communal one, if so desired. Thus, team discussions around "yesterday's service" or "the baptism," or conversations about Bible college and studies, could all (if appropriate) provide a catalyst for café-wide discussion and questions. Often, during my observations, it would be later, when the café busied up, that more intimate conversations and private enquiries took place. Occasionally, someone might request prayer, and a prayer session would move to the comfy sofas. Interestingly, this was not intrusive to those who preferred their own privacy. A busy café provides the perfect background noise for faith conversations. When interviewing the patrons, this came out several times:

> When I'd gone in to grab my baked potato, I did observe the local pastor was praying with somebody in the corner and someone had come in while I was waiting for my food, who was a little anxious and quite worried about something . . . and the way that the staff dealt with that person I thought, "Wow, this is just not an ordinary café. This is a place where people feel comfortable to come in and talk openly about what's troubling and worrying them." (Lucy)

> Because I think people, especially in an area like this, are going through so much in their lives anyway . . . so it's nice that if they choose to, then they can ask questions, they can have discussions. (Joselin)

Place can often be associated with simply the *physical*, the things we can touch. Yet also, we can speak of being in a "good place." This depicts an *emotional* location, too. The team in the Friendship Café were keen to provide an emotional location of peace, hope, and trust. The café manager, Lesley, told me:

> We needed to be, as I say, a neutral space where people could come, a safe space where we can express our faith. So that is what we do and how we care for people, but it is also very much so what we say and what we speak and what we talk about and how we operate in that space.

THE FRIENDSHIP CAFÉ AS KINGDOM

A Theology of the Kingdom is a helpful lens through which to view those Third Places run by faith-based organizations that have a gospel intentionality. When Jesus went about preaching and teaching, he spoke primarily of the Kingdom: the incoming rule and reign of God that he had started to usher in with his ministry (Luke 4:14–21). When Jesus sent out the disciples, their brief was one of proclamation and practice. They were to practically heal the sick while at the same time proclaim the inauguration of the Kingdom of God. The strategy was not about inviting people into a pre-sanctified space or place, but rather was one of procession and possession. They were to "go out" and "pronounce." Third Places provide great opportunities in the heart of our communities to demonstrate and declare the Kingdom of God. Kingdom work is progressive and relentless: an announcement, not a request. The very presence of God's people, incarnated in community place, praying over and proclaiming the rule and reign of King Jesus is a powerful thing. Within the previous section, comments from Lucy and Joselin demonstrated this observed progression: people seen praying, feeling a sense of peace and safety, comfortable to talk and share, yet all with a purpose, a gospel purpose.

THE GOSPEL OF THE FRIENDSHIP CAFÉ

The café management and team had stated all along that their objectives were two-fold: to develop a place that enhanced the local sense of community and to share the gospel. In an early interview, Lesley told me:

> I must say that each person is basically treated as an individual and we don't treat anyone any different from anybody else. So we will share our faith with whoever comes in through the door. I do get that probably some people in church would look at the marginalized as been more needy of the gospel, but actually everybody needs the gospel—whether they're in work or not.

Another one of the newer volunteers, Luke, told me:

> The ultimate goal is to see everyone that comes in come to faith but we are not bashing people over the heads with Bibles . . . there is no paraphernalia on the walls or anything to suggest it is church-run. It is more through conversations that people understand that we are a church run café.

There seemed to be a uniform understanding of the objectives throughout the café's team of volunteers. This mainly, as far as I could see, was due to the fact that the vast majority of the café team were already committed members and attendees of the parent

Whatever Happened to the Rich Young Man?

church. Some even possessed a more developed understanding of the missional strategy through their college studies. This synergy in the team was an essential aspect in the consistency of their message and the signature of the Friendship Café. This did not negate any individual personalities. Some were more comfortable with early, direct conversations about faith than others. Yet the collective witness was powerful and consistent. Feeling good about our own sense of purpose and achievement is one thing, but what about the all-important patrons? How did they feel? I was keen to find out about their experiences and how they felt about Christ being shared.

THE RESPONSE OF THE RICH YOUNG MAN

Cafés that operate as Third Places and do this well will attract a wide range of people demographics, and so it should be. This said, the research methods I used were designed to identify the New Marginalized so that I could find out how they felt about the Third Places they frequented, to the end that I could gauge its impact on their sense of community and their interest in matters of faith. Was it possible to balance these two aspects of community, well-being and faith-sharing? The responses of the patrons suggest that the balance between providing a welcoming, home-away-from-home community place, yet one with a gospel focus, had by and large been achieved in the Friendship Café. I saw this in a number of responses:

> I know if I wanted to come and talk about it (faith), I could and . . . it wouldn't be forced upon me. (Mike)
>
> Some people were praying in the corner. And people were coming in and feeling quite comfortable about that, and it had a really good feel that people weren't just, "Ugh, it's another place to go. Oh, it's church'!" It felt more than that, you know? It was the church reaching out into the community, but people felt that comfortability about speaking with people. (Lucy)
>
> Well, I don't think it [faith] is forced . . . it's just your own awareness of something . . . you've got to have that self-realization. (Annabelle)

A Tale of Two Cafés, Part 1: The Friendship Café

During my interviews and discussions with the café patrons, there was clearly what I would call an "invisible dynamic" or "trade-off" taking place within the hearts and minds of the patrons who frequented the café. This trade-off was between their overall appreciation of the café as a community place and their exposure to faith-based conversations. This reminds me a little of how I came to know Jesus. Each summer, my mother would send me to my uncle's home for a couple of weeks. This would break up the long school summer holidays for me (and my mother!). I used to love going to my uncle for those two weeks. He and his family were so much fun to be with. The only (initial) downside of it was that my uncle was an unashamed, passionate Christ-follower. He would share Jesus at every opportunity. While in the early years, I showed no real interest in this. The overall benefits and sheer fun of being with my uncle and his family was a trade-off I was happy to make. In a similar way, for my research into the two cafés, I wanted to know whether it was possible for a community of passionate Christ-followers to make such a difference in their communities—and whether any faith-sharing that the patrons experienced was a price off-set by their love of being a part of such a community.

This all said, I also sensed within some of the conversations and interviews that the patrons appreciated the balance within the café. The fact that the staff were not "over the top" but rather relied on natural faith-sharing opportunities was key. While the development of a valued, community place would seem to mitigate significantly with regard to any faith-sharing, ongoing sensitivity to Spirit-given opportunities would still be needed.

My time spent in the Friendship Café was both encouraging and insightful. There was hope for the rich young man without doubt. Indeed, as a postscript to this section, in 2018, Lucy the youth worker started to attend the main Sunday services at Phoenix Church. In 2019, she was baptized. Just as Luke gives us the encouraging account of Zacchaeus following the rich young man narrative, salvation had come to Lucy's house, too.

Chapter 6

A Tale of Two Cafés, Part 2: The Welcome Café

The Welcome Café was established in 2009 and is located within a busy and thriving community center in the Bourneville area of Birmingham, UK. The café and community center are collectively run by a charitable trust. This trust was set up by Gateway Church in 1996, with the church also meeting within the community center. Thus, there are strong links between the church, the café, and the overall community center trust board. Gateway Church is also based in an evangelical tradition and originally was the sole source of volunteers for the café when it was established in 2009. Since then, the busy café has taken on paid management and staff to run and develop it. My early conversations with the café and community center managers revealed that they had joint objectives for the café to be a place that enhanced community while, at the same time, provided a platform from which to share their faith in Christ. The striking and immediate difference between the Welcome Café and the Friendship Café is found in their geographical locations and also their overall patron "footfall." The Welcome Café is located within an affluent area of Birmingham. It sits within a community center that acts as a hub for local families. With picturesque surroundings and outer grounds, including a lake for fishing, the Welcome Café, particularly in the summer, provides an idyllic location for a Third Place. Additionally, on observation, the patron footfall is significant, with many young families accessing the café throughout the day. My general conversations also revealed a patronage with a greater proportion of disposable income. This provided a rich vein of patrons to help me with my research. Yet, as per the previous chapter, before I wade into any sociological and theological findings, it would be good and polite to introduce the people first.

THE PEOPLE OF THE WELCOME CAFÉ

I had frequented the café prior to my research. The Bible college where I taught was located within the same building. I was a regular patron at the café well before I was a researcher! I had gotten to know some of the staff on a polite level, often exchanging general chat about the college, the café, and the weather. Once I started my research, I was keen to meet the café management and gauge what their objectives were for the café. During one of my lunchtime visits, I was introduced to Katy, the café manager. I briefly gave her an outline of my research and asked if it would be possible to chat to her more formally about the café's objectives. Katy agreed. We arranged a separate meeting during which Katy shared the vision:

> We're operating on a community basis with Christian values and using opportunities to share the fact that we are Christians . . . we see it very much as bringing people in, giving people the option, opening those conversations, making people aware of what's going on in the church, making absolutely everything we do makes people aware that it's because we are Christians.

Katy was passionate about the café and often, during our conversation, referred back to the "original" vision back in 2009 when the café was set up and run by volunteers from Gateway Church. Katy expressed that in recent years the café had somewhat "lost its focus," and so her role was to bring that focus back. Rather like the Friendship Café, the Welcome Café's (stated) purpose was to develop a

Whatever Happened to the Rich Young Man?

local Third Place with a gospel intentionality—objectives that Katy realistically recognized were still very much a work in progress.

THE TEAM

The staff at the Welcome Café comprised both paid employees and volunteers. This provided an interesting mix, but I'll go into more of that later in the chapter. I was able to speak to a number of staff, but not all. However, what was clear from my general interactions with the staff was that they all seemed to enjoy the environment they were in. The main days I frequented the café were Thursdays (my lecturing days) and some Tuesdays (for the occasional staff meeting). Thus, I got to the know the teams on those shifts quite well, with several of them forming the staff's contributions for my research interviews.

THE PATRONS

The patrons were generally varied; however, there was a noticeable demographic of stay at home mums that frequented the café. Sarah was an architect who worked three days a week and brought her preschool child to the café each Thursday to meet up with other mums and their children. Louise was another mum who had stopped work as a teacher to raise her young family. Jane was a primary school teacher who worked part-time but was also heavily involved with the community center, being on the board of trustees. Jane had school-aged children and so could now give more time to her work and trustee duties. Dave worked in the community center offices in IT support. He would frequently spend his lunchtimes and breaks in the café. Additionally, there were other groups of people who would use the café as their meeting place: a local book club and a running club, amongst others. Overall, this was a thriving center for the community. The patrons seemed relaxed and happy to be there. The staff/patron interactions, from what I could see, were polite and friendly. This looked promising. Of course, the research would reveal the depths to which those relationships went.

A Tale of Two Cafés, Part 2: The Welcome Café

THE PRODUCTS OF THE WELCOME CAFÉ

To enhance the polite and friendly staff, the Welcome Café itself was warm and welcoming. It was much larger than the Friendship Café. It was able to seat around forty-five patrons at any time. There was a large, inviting display of freshly made cakes and other bakes, all freshly prepared on site. These were well-presented in a glass case that patrons could browse while in the queue waiting to be served. The menu differed in that it did not offer the traditional full English breakfast. Rather, there were a range of homemade soups, freshly made sandwiches, toasties, and cakes. Drinks were varied with a range of hot drinks using a higher-end coffee-producing machine, providing a range of coffees, hot chocolate, with a refrigerator containing a range of cold drinks. The quality of the food was high, though the waiting times were typically much longer than in the Friendship Café. Again, this was down to the volume of patron traffic. Early conversations within the café certainly outlined these essential "people and place" aspects positively:

> It's just a comfortable environment. It's not too new and tidy. I feel like the kids can roam about and can do stuff. (Sarah)
>
> I would say it's brilliant. It's really nice having the park but it's just friendly and welcoming. . .it's not the most glamorous place, but it's a place where people feel comfortable so it's quite down to earth. (Liz)

This all said, although the Welcome Café had identical objectives to the Friendship Café, its high volume and busy environment gave it a different feel. In my initial observations, I wondered: *How might this affect any of the staff's interactions with patrons?* More on that later.

THE WELCOME CAFÉ AS SOCIOLOGICAL PLACE

In chapter 4, we outlined the various sociological factors impacting *place* using Waxman's categories of cleanliness, appealing aroma,

Whatever Happened to the Rich Young Man?

adequate lighting, comfortable furniture, and a view to the outside.[1] In chapter 5, we assessed these within the Friendship Café. This section will now consider the same within the Welcome Café.

The location of the Welcome Café, both geographically in a picturesque part of Bourneville, plus its central location within a busy community center, makes it an ideal initiative to be developed into a Third Place. The café has a constant "buzz" to it with a consistent and regular throughput of patrons. The surrounding grounds, with the lake as its centerpiece, enhance the overall experience. The café itself is clean and well-presented. Music plays in the background and the food and serving counters are well-presented. The lighting is good, though no real "mood" lighting is available; this does not detract from an overall impression of a good, busy, local café. Seating is generic wooden café chairs. These aren't especially comfortable, but their look is homely. The wooden tables match. Collectively, the furniture gives the impression of a cottage. A couple of small comfy sofas in one of the café corners provide the seating for a small toy area designed to keep children entertained. Within the café itself, there are windows on one side that give a lovely view out to the lake. Additional seating outside completes the physical aspects, collectively going above and beyond Waxman's five categories of physical factors that contribute to place attachment. Several of the patrons interviewed commented:

> I would say it's a lovely, rough-and-ready, open, welcoming place. Don't come here if you're expecting super-duper, slick customer service and posh coffees and all of that . . . like a kind of Starbucks experience, but if you're looking for a place that's part of the community, that's real, that's authentic, you know where you can have a chat and there's always someone to talk to, it's just a welcoming, friendly place. (Sue)

> So in places like Costa, you feel like if you haven't got a coffee, you're frowned at, you know? And you need to move on because the next one's coming in. I don't feel that here. I feel like you're just welcome to have a bit of time out, if that's what you want. (Sarah)

1. Waxman, "The Coffee Shop."

A Tale of Two Cafés, Part 2: The Welcome Café

So, regarding Third-Place *physical* factors, the Welcome Café looks promising. The constant hustle and bustle of the café, with many regular and recognized faces, all bode well for a welcoming home away from home where people feel comfortable. All high scoring requirements of any would-be Third Place. Just to conclude this section, and our sociological considerations, what about the machinery?

THE MACHINERY OF THE WELCOME CAFÉ

The Welcome Café coffee-producing equipment needed to be able to handle the higher demand of its patrons. The dual-cup machine was constantly in use, to the extent that a four-cup machine would probably be kept busy, too! The delay in producing hot drinks was one of the trade-offs the patrons recognized but tolerated. Sue's comments (above) about not expecting "super-duper slick service" captured this. In my experiences, if my time was restricted due to a limited lunch break, waiting ten-to-fifteen minutes for your order was sometimes a challenge. This did not seem to be an issue for the majority of the patrons who valued the other aspects of this Third Place, such as quality of conversation, location, quality of food, and so on. The location of the coffee-producing machine (again) meant baristas had their backs to the patrons during preparation, but like the Friendship Café, a "delivery to table" service was offered to counter this.

As we conclude our sociological considerations of the Welcome Café, it would be easy to surmise that this was a thriving Third Place, and in sociological terms, it was. The busyness and loyalty of regular customers testified to that fact. However, who were having these Third-Place conversations? What was the staff's overall view? What about those joint objectives of developing a Third Place that both enhanced community and served as a platform for faith-based conversations? We need to let theology join the conversation now, in order to give us these insights.

Whatever Happened to the Rich Young Man?

THE WELCOME CAFÉ AS THEOLOGICAL PLACE

We already established in previous chapters that "all spaces and places" are the Lord's (Ps 24:1). So in that sense, as a place, the same can be applied to the Welcome Café as per any other place. However, I mentioned also previously that over the centuries there has been a movement toward categorizing places into *sacred* and *secular*. Thus, many Christian projects prefer to adopt strategies that ensure their places can be clearly identified as *sacred*. The ultimate strategy is to, of course, locate our project within an identifiable church building. Yet increasing community suspicions around institutionalized religion might seriously hamper such projects if community outreach is the objective. Both the Friendship Café and the Welcome Café occupy places in the hearts of their respective communities, and so the question then becomes how they might differentiate themselves as sacred places where the glory and worship of God is a desired aim.

For the Friendship Café, I observed that there was very little in the way of overt Christian artifacts or icons to communicate the café's identity. It was the volunteers who saw themselves as differentiating their community by acting as "living letters" (2 Cor 3:2). So what about the Welcome Café? How did they communicate their identity? How did the staff see their role within this? Regarding visible identifiers, the Welcome Café had a number of low-key displays and items that communicated their faith-based roots. A chalkboard as you entered the café had a verse of Scripture written on it. On the serving counter, as patrons waited to be served or to pay, there were welcome cards that, if so desired, could be filled in to facilitate deeper inquiry or connection. One significant visible strategy was reserved for Sundays when the café took on a different "feel." As the Gateway Church would be holding its services in the same building, the café would be used as an outlet for church members. This placed the initiative firmly in the hands of the faith community and provided opportunities for patrons to see what goes on during a Sunday service. This "Sunday café" signature was also augmented by two important aspects: free tea and coffee for all patrons and the opportunity to request prayer. Katy, the café manager, explained:

A Tale of Two Cafés, Part 2: The Welcome Café

It was decided that we would open the café on Sundays—as we now give free tea and coffee from the church on a Sunday for a couple of hours—and that is very much a mission on a Sunday. So the café, even on a Sunday, is very much about presence evangelism and very much we don't want barriers between the church and the people. We also found that people didn't know there was a church there, though they came to the toddler groups in the week. Also, we have the opportunity for prayer, we have prayer sheets and a prayer book, and staff are encourage to ask people if they would like prayer.

It was clear through my conversations with Katy that Sunday was very different in the café. It seemed this was their set-aside opportunity. I wondered why this was. This was borne out during my conversation with Sarah. Sarah had been attending the café for eight years, yet also recognized the different feel on Sundays:

> If you come on a Sunday morning, then it does have a religious feel, because the church is on a Sunday morning, and they open the café after church, on a Sunday morning, so it's just the people that are here for that event.

Sarah tended to use "other" language when it came to describing Sundays. This was an interesting development within my conversation with Sarah, as up to that point she had aired a real sense of ownership on the café. In fact, Sarah was quite protective of what she saw as "her little café," not only regarding Sundays, but also when other events took over the site:

> I don't want it to be a victim of its own success. I like it the way it is. I want to keep it local for the local community. They do fireworks night and they have fairgrounds and stuff. And to be honest I don't really like that.

I was beginning to wonder about the conversations and connections between the staff and patrons like Sarah. Sarah loved the community feel of the café, but when I observed her, she was speaking to other regular patrons. Indeed, referring back to the overall busyness of the café, the staff hardly had time to engage in meaningful conversations. Perhaps Sundays changed this, as the ratios of

Whatever Happened to the Rich Young Man?

patrons to those from a faith background willing to converse were significantly different. But as opportunity did arise in the busy weekdays, what did the café's staff feel about the objectives? Were they prepared and willing to share and show Christ? Was providing a foretaste of the Kingdom a priority? My conversations with them would reveal this.

THE WELCOME CAFÉ AS KINGDOM

Reminding ourselves of Newbigin's words, he saw the gathering of God's people as the true hermeneutic of the gospel.[2] Meaning that if we truly want to see and experience a taste of the Kingdom, then there is no better witness to this than a group of Christ-followers who model what it means to serve King Jesus. In chapter 4, we also saw the importance of gaining the right balance within our teams, between those who align themselves with the gospel and the Kingdom-vision, and those who perhaps are on a journey of "belonging before you believe." I remind the reader of these words because, during my staff interviews with the team of the Welcome Café, it became obvious that this was not the case. My early interview and discussions with Katy (the café manager), had hinted at such. She had echoed her desire to get back to the original vision of 2009. Added to this, the quantitative questionnaires that I initially gave out to help identify the New Marginalized demographic also gave room for participants to indicate any faith-based conversations they had been involved with. There was a noticeable absence in the vast majority of cases. The building picture may help us to see why the espoused objectives of building community and gospel intentionality were so at odds in this Third Place. Regarding a sense of community, the Welcome Café operated as an outstanding Third Place. It was the second associated objective, that of engaging in gospel conversations, that had been diluted. As I conducted my interviews and observed the interactions within the café, I could broadly put this down to two things: The constant busyness and the demands of patrons reduced any opportunity for sharing, plus

2. Newbigin, *The Gospel in a Pluralist Society*, 227.

A Tale of Two Cafés, Part 2: The Welcome Café

the disconnect between the management vision and many of the staff team. Sundays gave a glimmer of hope regarding how things could be; additionally, within the busyness of the café, there were some encouraging signs that in spite of the barriers to fulfilling the vision, that God was at work, anyway. Considering my interviews with staff, Jodie and Becky demonstrated this diluted challenge. Firstly, I asked Jodie what she felt about the faith-sharing vision of the café management:

> It's their café. They can do what they want. They're higher than us, but I'd probably want to understand why. Does that mean you wouldn't want a certain people coming in and what would you do with all of us because the majority of us who work in the café aren't Christian. We don't have, I don't think, any beliefs, apart from a few.

Yet in speaking to Becky:

> We want to provide good service, good coffee, good food for the community, for the people that come through here, but more so on a deeper level, it's just serving the community, like, it's all about serving but, like serving with that faith and serving others like Christ served them and you know, that selfless nature. It's really interesting when you have people who aren't connected to church or aren't Christians, I mean, it's easy to ask, to ask people to be a nice person, to be kind and stuff like that, so I don't think that's a big ask of people, but doing it on behalf of the church or because we are connected to the church or because our objectives are Christian, I think it's interesting sometimes asking people almost to subscribe to those things when actually they don't believe in God.

Becky was passionate about sharing the vision, but clearly saw a tension between this and co-laboring alongside those team members that did not share this vision. Becky herself was still working out what she felt was the best approach and how this tension between building a great Third-Place community and faith-sharing might work:

Whatever Happened to the Rich Young Man?

I know that a lot of people have different opinions on how we are doing on this. Some people think we're barely doing anything and we should be doing so much more, and other people think that actually we're being a little bit too much in people's faces. So, it is interesting to see the spectrum of that. I think the key time when that happens (faith-sharing) is a Sunday morning. We actually have volunteers from the Church that come in and give free tea and coffee to the community on a Sunday morning, and it's become such an awesome, special thing that happens because you get to say, "Hey, here's a free cup of coffee. It's from the church. Have a great day." And the patrons will say, "Oh my gosh," and, you know, it starts off really cool conversations: "Oh my goodness, like, thank you so much, why are you doing this? Are you sure I can't give you any money?"

Also, we're able to offer people the opportunity to write down a prayer request or even pray with people and, again, it's that relationship-building. I'm a big believer in relationships, all of those things, and so relational faith, really. I think that—in my opinion, or at least that's what works best for me—bringing people to Christ starts with building a relationship first. You can't just put up a poster or say something or shove a Bible in someone's face. It starts with a relationship and so, I think, in that way, Sunday morning has been really, really special. We (also) have a Wednesday communion service and we're able to actually take those prayer requests from Sunday morning and pray for them, and so I think that is a really, really special way. We're also getting ready to do an Alpha course, and so we've been gently promoting that in here, literally just through posters but that's the biggest way that it's done. I don't actually think it (faith-sharing) happens much through the week other than if, one of the ministers pops into the café and starts having a conversation with someone or one of the members of the church that come in, or I actually get to have some fun conversations because I'm not from here, and so people will say, "Why are you here?" and so I get to say, "I work for a church, you know, this is why I'm here"—and so, I personally get to have some fun

A Tale of Two Cafés, Part 2: The Welcome Café

conversations about faith and inviting people to church in that way, and so that's it."

With so much variation in the staff team's understanding and approach to the café's vision, then the impact on any such collective signature is obvious. In many ways, this broad and varied interaction worked with regard to community impact. In addition, it could be argued that the varied staff and volunteer team also, in itself, provided a mission field for friendship and gospel-sharing. The question here would be to ask: Has the right balance been achieved? I mentioned earlier that with regard to the patrons, they are more than likely not to differentiate between those staff who follow Christ and those who do not. The Welcome Café's strong association with the church would make this a challenge as varied worldviews on life, death, marriage, sexuality, and so on would be held and eventually shared. Ultimately, what this impacts is the gospel signature of our organization as conflicting values and allegiances are displayed or expressed.

THE GOSPEL OF THE WELCOME CAFÉ

It would be easy to have read to this point and think that the Welcome Café was not fulfilling its stated vision. The encouraging thing about my time in the café, and my conversations with the patrons, was that in the midst of the busyness, team dysfunction, and misaligned team vision, God was at work. He often works in spite of us and not because of. Without doubt, as Katy identified and expressed only too well, there was a need to get back to the original 2009 gospel vision; however, there were some encouraging shoots of hope: the Sunday morning experience, where patrons requested prayer, the recognition within the weekly café that it was being run by a faith-based organization, the conversations within the staff team about church and faith, conversations with visiting interns from the US that sparked interest in faith and Christ following, and an overall sense that this was a home-away-from-home place where people would feel welcome and conversations could take place. Additionally, while my research may have exposed some hidden

Whatever Happened to the Rich Young Man?

tensions around vision and gospel sharing, these were, I would suggest, invisible to the patrons who frequented the Welcome Café. But what did they think about the café as a faith community? How did they feel about any faith conversations they had been involved with or overheard?

THE RESPONSE OF THE RICH YOUNG MAN

It was clear from all of my conversations with the patrons that they loved the café. Many felt a strong sense of ownership and belonging. Place attachment was evident. If the previous findings from the Friendship Café were anything to go by, this bodes well for fulfilling the broader vision of faith-sharing. Such conversations based upon a platform of Third-Place relationships can be held in healthy tension. The patrons of the Welcome Café were happy to share their views:

> I think it's doing amazingly because I think a lot of people . . . even if people don't know that this is related to a church (you kind of do from some little bits . . . like the words on the blackboard and stuff), but to me, I think it's got a feeling of, like, being a blessed place. That's how I feel. I'm not a Christian myself, but I feel like it feels like a blessing—a special place. When people come here, it feels like home and people feel relaxed and I think people who are lonely and things like that can just come here and meet other people, speak to the staff, but also feel better for having been here. (Jane)

> I struggle sometimes with what I do and don't believe in, but I still keep coming back here because it's an anchor, and I think that's part of what they do as part of the café. It's an anchor, and you can see that by the way they're living and the way that they include everybody, serve everybody. I think it opens the doors for people if they want to ask questions, then they can. It's not put in their faces. And they're shown that it's a lived experience which I think, for me, gives me something to hold on to in my faith. Because if you can see how it's worked out and how people serve in this community, if you can see

A Tale of Two Cafés, Part 2: The Welcome Café

how people live it, it gives me a bit of hope for how I do it too. (Gemma)

Work in progress would be a good description for the Welcome Café. The challenge in the months ahead would be to discern how they might strengthen and unify the collective team vision and impact the overall gospel signature of this thriving Third Place. The rich young man was frequenting the café, and although he was loving what went on (with regard to community), he still had some unanswered questions:

> It's interesting, actually. I was speaking to someone here once (a believer), when something happened that I was a bit thrown by, and I just happened to say to this person, "This has happened"—and I wouldn't have minded a faith perspective on that, but they didn't give that, or didn't overtly give that. And I remember thinking, "Oh, actually, I wouldn't have minded if you had brought a bit more of your faith into that conversation." Generally, when I come and ask for advice, I'm really open-minded and I think, I'm never going to be close. (Marie)

My overall sense, as I spoke to patrons in general, is that within the right atmosphere, in those God-given moments, at the right time, as God's people discern, people are more open to talk about Christ than what we may think. Anna Strhan in her book *Aliens and Strangers?* speaks about "imagined barriers."[3] These are self-constructed barriers of doubt, fear of failure, and even disbelief—all leading to a net approach that believes that the rich young men, the presenting self-sufficient, the New Marginalized, simply do not want to know. I want to strongly challenge this assumption and encourage the reader that throughout my research in these two amazing cafés, there was a thirst and desire from many such patrons who were still asking, "What must I do to inherit eternal life" (Luke 18:18)?

---

3. Strhan, *Aliens and Strangers?*, 4.

Chapter 7

Theological Reflection and Conclusions

While our considerations up to now have brought both a theological and sociological perspective on the church's engagement with the New Marginalized, it is important from an evangelical perspective that the theology and, more specifically, the Bible, have the last word. I hope this book has given some helpful insights and practical examples on how the local church can engage with the non-welfare demographic that all too often presents itself as self-sufficient. Within this final chapter, we will go back to our core source, the Bible, beginning with Luke 19 and the narrative of Zacchaeus. In the classic film, *The Wizard of Oz*, the heroine Dorothy discovered that the answers she was looking for had been there all along. I would affirm that this is also true for the Christ-follower who holds to the tenet that the Bible informs the whole of life and is indeed a "light for our path" (Ps 119:105).

SO IS IT REALLY IMPOSSIBLE?

In chapter 1, I briefly summarized the narrative of the rich young man from Luke 18. I suggested that the key understanding of that

Theological Reflection and Conclusions

narrative hinged on the difference between something being difficult [*duskolos*] or impossible [*adynata*]. Confusing these two can lead to difficult and challenging things being communicated as impossible things. This, I would suggest, has happened when it comes to, not only our understanding of Luke 18, but our approach to engaging the non-welfare demographic in general. As a result, they have become the New Marginalized. Many within the church allow *imagined* barriers to disable their strategy and everyday connections with society's "self-sufficient." This being the case, we can also allow the Bible to deconstruct such barriers. Indeed, Luke does this for us in his very next chapter, in the account of Zacchaeus.

Luke chapter 19 commences with Jesus [*Yeshua/Joshua*] entering the ancient city of Jericho (Luke 19:1). Now, the very mention of the name of that city might cause us to reflect upon another Joshua. Joshua 6 gives us the account of Joshua seeking to enter the city of Jericho, a great walled city. The great walls of the city were a barrier to Joshua and the people, but armed with God's strategy, they were able to overcome. What is impossible with man is possible with God. Back to Luke 19, having just pronounced the difficulty of engaging with the materially self-sufficient, Luke tells us:

> Jesus entered Jericho and was passing through. A man was there by the name of Zacchaeus; he was a chief tax collector and was wealthy. (Luke 19:1–2)

This time in Jericho, the pronounced barriers are different. While Jesus is welcomed into the city with great crowds, Zacchaeus, a wealthy man, is amongst them. In addition to this, Zacchaeus would have his own barriers to overcome. As a tax collector, he would be despised by his own people, seen by many as colluding with the Roman authorities. He effectively benefited from the enforced occupation. Luke also tells us of a physical barrier Zacchaeus had, his height: "[Zacchaeus] wanted to see who Jesus was, but because he was short, he could not see over the crowd" (Luke 19:3). Many people have their own daily struggles and barriers to face. The materially self-sufficient are not exempt from this. Stories of high profile celebrity suicides are testimony to this fact.

Whatever Happened to the Rich Young Man?

Having said this, Luke tells us that there was a determination within Zacchaeus to see Jesus: "So he ran ahead and climbed a sycamore fig tree to see him, since Jesus was coming that way" (Luke 19:4). In my years of serving both within industry and paid ministry, it is my experience that many people within this demographic have questions about life and are searching. Many have their own daily struggles and barriers. God places his people strategically and specifically, as his ambassadors, to help them find the answer. Jesus models this in Luke 19:

> When Jesus reached the spot, he looked up and said to him, "Zacchaeus, come down immediately, I must stay at your house today." So, he came down at once and welcomed him gladly. (Luke 19:5–6)

Following this encounter with Jesus, Zacchaeus is transformed. Any dependence he may have had on his wealth or status takes second place. In spite of the criticisms of the onlooking crowd who are unable to see past their own prejudice toward Zacchaeus (verse 7), Luke tells us:

> Zacchaeus stood up and said to the Lord, "Look, Lord! Here and now I give half of my possessions to the poor, and if I have cheated anybody out of anything, I will pay back four times the amount." (Luke 19:8)

While the Old Testament law demanded recompense of four or five times the amount in cases of cheating and usury (Ex 22:1; 2 Sam 12:9), Zacchaeus' transformation went far beyond the requirements of the law. This direct encounter with Jesus had unlocked Zacchaeus' heart and allegiance, which he expressed in his immediate giving away of half of his possessions, in addition to seeking to honor God's Word. As this visible fruit of transformation is witnessed, Jesus declares, "Today, salvation has come to this house, because this man, too, is a son of Abraham. For the Son of Man came to seek and to save the lost" (Luke 19:9–10). As we encounter the New Marginalized within our spheres of influence, our central desire must be that they might have a direct and life-changing encounter with Jesus. All too often, we might substitute this with an invitation

Theological Reflection and Conclusions

to a church event or service. We have seen that Third Places run by Christ-followers passionate about the gospel can create ideal places of encounter. Of course, God is not restricted to the development of Third Places. Our individual effectiveness in the varied locations we find ourselves is equally as valid and essential.

THE IMPACT OF YEAST: A KINGDOM INFLUENCE

Within the Third-Place case studies in chapters 5–6, we saw that both the Friendship Café and the Welcome Café sought to create places that might give a foretaste of the Kingdom to come. While the patrons within each café had varying exposures to faith-based conversations (or not), what was common was the sense that they were in a "blessed place." The conversations validated what the patrons saw amongst the staff and what they felt in these places.

When it comes to describing the Kingdom of God and its progressive influence, the Bible gives us plenty of material directly from the teachings of Jesus himself. In chapter 4 of Mark's Gospel, Jesus describes the Kingdom as a "grain seed" and a "mustard seed" (Mark 4:26–32). Both of these pictures speak to us about the small but progressive nature of God's Kingdom: "All by itself the soil produces grain—first the stalk, and then the head, then the full kernel in the head" (Mark 4:28). In the early stages, the growth may seem insignificant; however, the Kingdom influence becomes increasingly visible:

> Yet when planted, it grows and becomes the largest of all garden plants, with such big branches that the birds can perch in it shade. (Mark 4:32)

This imagery of an influential and thriving kingdom would not have been lost on those listening to Jesus. In various places within the Old Testament, we see the rise and fall of kingdoms described in such terms:

> On the mountain heights of Israel I will plant it; it will produce branches and bear fruit and become a splendid cedar. Birds of every kind will nest in it; they will find shelter in the shade of its branches. (Ezek 17:23)

Whatever Happened to the Rich Young Man?

> All the birds of the sky nested in its boughs, all the animals of the wild gave birth under its branches; all the great nations lived in its shade. (Ezek 31:6)
>
> With beautiful leaves and abundant fruit, providing food for all, giving shelter to the wild animals, and having nesting places in its branches for the birds. (Dan 4:21)

All of this would give more of a progressive picture as opposed to a one-off cataclysmic event. Additionally, Jesus could use other metaphors depicting the widespread and progressive nature and influence of the Kingdom of God:

> Again Jesus asked, "What shall I compare the kingdom of God to? It is like yeast that a woman took and mixed into about sixty pounds of flour until it worked all through the dough." (Luke 13:20-21)

This imagery of yeast and how it "works its way through the dough" is an interesting one for us to ponder. There are several aspects of yeast that might inform our understanding and strategy of what it means to be "Kingdom influencers." Yeast has no real impact when it is clumped together or remains in its packaging. Yeast is most effective as it is allowed to maximize its influence. There is no hierarchy in yeast: each part simply influences the part of the dough it is in and then works its way through. Yeast has the capacity to spoil, too. Indeed, in many parts of Scripture, it is seen as a negative influence (Ex 12:1-20; Ex 23:18). Jesus also used the imagery of yeast as a picture of the negative teaching of the Pharisees (Matt 16:6), as did the Apostle Paul when he exhorted the Corinthian church to guard against the "yeast" of immorality and boasting (1 Cor 5:1-8).

Considering these collective pictures and texts, for the Christ-follower desiring to be a Kingdom influence today, the parallels are striking. The strategy of remaining within our gathered "safe places" is not the most effective one. It has limited impact on our communities. As Kingdom "yeast," God's people need permission to exercise as widespread an influence as possible, being equipped and encouraged within the specific "batch of dough" they are located. Any hierarchies (beyond equipping) that are unhelpful and

Theological Reflection and Conclusions

restrictive need dismantling in order to release the "yeast" into the "dough." God's people also have the capacity to be a negative influence, too—be it through their words, teachings, or behaviors.

SO WHAT ARE WE WAITING FOR?

Having presented the case for the New Marginalized, and shown how both sociology and theology can inform Third Places that are driven by a gospel intentionality, and having encouraged each Christ-follower to see themselves as influential Kingdom yeast, the question must now be asked: *So what are we waiting for?* Of course, the reticence of God's people to put into practice Christ's command to go is well-rehearsed. Following the Great Commission in Matthew 28, the disciples are still happy to "wait," prioritizing their own close fellowship (as necessary as that is).[1] It takes the increased persecution of the believers in Acts 8 to cause them to disperse out of their familiar gatherings. The difference with regard to the challenge of this book is that as Christ-followers today, our commission is two-fold: the call to enter our communities and develop those Third Places conducive to community-building and meaningful conversation; but also the call to realize that many of us are already interacting with the New Marginalized in our current day-to-day lives. Rather than seeing those around us, both inside and outside of any Third Place, as "targets" for evangelism, our call is to see people as "objects" of God's love. Be it as individuals or small groups and pockets of believers, our Kingdom-influence will be progressive. We can ask the Holy Spirit to deconstruct any barriers within those that he connects us with; in turn, we can ask him to deconstruct any imagined barriers that we or the enemy of souls might place within us. The rich young man is still asking questions, still seeking, still wanting to know. Yet whatever barriers are presented, real or imagined, and however difficult the situation may be, with God all things are possible.

---

1. Acts 2:42–47 outlines the disciple's practice of meeting together around the four tenets of the Apostles: teaching, fellowship, prayer, and the breaking of bread.

Appendix: Questions for Reflection

INTRODUCTION

This section is designed for either individual or group study. The recommended method would be to read a chapter at a time, then reflect on the corresponding chapter questions in this section. The questions are not exhaustive but are designed to encourage deeper thinking, discussion, and ultimately action! May the Lord richly bless you in your endeavors.

CHAPTER 1 REFLECTIONS

a. To what extent do you feel your church and everyday life are connected, be it at work, home, etc.?
b. How have you shared (or shown) your faith to those who present themselves as self-sufficient?
c. To what extent (if any) has the church generally ignored the New Marginalized? Do you think the assessment in chapter 1 is fair?

Appendix: Questions for Reflection

CHAPTER 2 REFLECTIONS

a. To what extent should the local church respond to the measured needs of their communities?
b. What might be some "unmeasured" needs in local communities that are much more subjective?
c. What perceptions might the people living in the community around your local church have of your church's role and purpose?
d. Do you think it is possible for the church to unashamedly possess a gospel intentionality yet keep its place at the "community table"?

CHAPTER 3 REFLECTIONS

a. According to Newbigin, there is nothing more powerful than a community of God's people when it wants to demonstrate to a watching world what it truly means to be a child of the King and a citizen of his Kingdom. To what extent do you agree with this?
b. Think about *your* favorite Third Place. Why do you like it so much?
c. What Third Places near your church/home do you frequent? If it was possible, what sort of Third Place might be good for your church to create?
d. To what extent should churches seek to *incarnate* within their local communities as a progressive Kingdom presence? Do you feel churches should create "alternative sacred spaces" within their facilities in which to invite people?
e. Tim Chester describes "gospel-less" projects as "signposts pointing nowhere." Do you agree with this? Why or why not?

Appendix: Questions for Reflection

CHAPTER 4 REFLECTIONS

a. This chapter tells a little story of a "less than satisfactory" visit to a café. Have you had a similar experience? How did it make you feel?
b. A *belonging-before-you-believe* approach seeks to involve "not-yet-believers" in Christian projects in the hope that they might be influenced by the broader team of believers. What has been *your* experience of this? Do you think this is a good thing? What are the benefits and risks?
c. How important is it that each staff member within a ministry project shares the vision of the project? With pressure on rota, to keep going, et al—what is often the reality of this?
d. How important is it that the product or service offered by the church or ministry is the best it can be?
e. Which of the other *sociological* factors of a successful Third Place, in this chapter, resonated with you (lighting, machinery, cleanliness, aroma, furniture, etc.)?
f. Thinking about the section under the heading "Mars Hill Café," how are we entering our local marketplaces of discussion and debate?

CHAPTER 5 REFLECTIONS

a. Thinking about the objectives of the management teams of both cafés, to what extent do you think it is possible to hold both objectives (i.e., enhancing a sense of local community with a gospel intentionality) in tension?
b. Do you think it is necessary to have a gospel intentionality? Can't such places as The Friendship Café and The Welcome Café simply desire to bless the local community?
c. What was your reaction to the research in The Friendship Café? Did anything surprise you?
d. To what extent were both the sociological and theological aspects of the café important?

Appendix: Questions for Reflection

e. What might be the pros and cons of either a café located within the community or one located within its own church building?

CHAPTER 6 REFLECTIONS

a. What where the most striking differences between The Welcome Café and The Friendship Café?
b. To what extent might The Welcome Café be a victim of its own success? In what ways?
c. How might Katy go about realigning the vision of the staff team?
d. Neither café had large amounts of material that displayed their faith-based roots. To what extent might this help or hinder their objectives?
e. The Welcome Café used its Sunday church service as an opportunity to give the café a different "feel." What are your thoughts on this strategy? Do you think this should be the Monday-to-Saturday norm, too?
f. To what extent would the existence of a mixed staff team of Christ-followers and not-yet-believers be a mission field in itself?
g. During one of the interviews, Marie expressed how, in one situation, she would have liked one of the Christians within the café to have shared their faith perspective, and was sad this did not happen. In what ways has this challenged you to discern when the Holy Spirit might be at work in your everyday conversations?
h. This chapter also speaks about *imagined barriers*. How might this be true for both Christ-followers and those within our communities? What sorts of barriers might each group face, both real and imaginary?

Appendix: Questions for Reflection

CHAPTER 7 REFLECTIONS

a. "Many people have their own daily struggles and barriers to face. The materially self-sufficient are not exempt from this." Think about this quote from chapter 7. What sorts of barriers and struggles might these be?
b. Discuss this quote: "As we encounter the New Marginalized within our spheres of influence, our central desire must be that they might have a direct, life-changing encounter with Jesus. All too often, we might substitute this with an invitation to a church event or service."
c. This chapter describes the Christ-follower's influence as a "progressive Kingdom yeast." Which qualities of yeast most resonated with you?
d. Think about or discuss how the principles discussed in this book might impact your everyday life and ministry practices.

Bibliography

Augustine. *The Confessions.* Translated by Edward Bouverie Pusey. Franklin Center, PA: Franklin Library, 1982.

Baker, Chris. "Spiritual Capital and Progressive Localism." *Public Spirit* (blog), February 2014. http://www.publicspirit.org.uk/spiritual-capital-and-progressive-localism/.

Beaumont, Justin, and Christ Baker, eds. *Postsecular Cities: Space, Theory and Practice.* London: Continuum, 2011.

Bebbington, D.W. *Evangelicalism in Modern Britain: A History from the 1730s to the 1980s.* London: Routledge, 2005.

Chester, Tim. *Good News to the Poor: Social Involvement and the Gospel.* Nottingham, UK: InterVarsity, 2004.

Cloke, Paul, et al. *Working Faith: Faith-based Organizations and Urban Social Justice.* Milton Keynes, UK: Paternoster, 2013.

Graham, Elaine, and Stephen Lowe. *What Makes a Good City? Public Theology and the Urban Church.* London: Darton, Longman & Todd, 2009.

Foss, Kelci, and Stephanie Saey. "The Third Place Experience in Urban and Rural Coffee Shops." *MJUR* 6 (2016) 171–77.

Foster, Keith, and Andrew R. Hardy. *Body and Blood: The Body of Christ in the Life of the Community.* Eugene, OR: Cascade, 2019.

Harries, Richard. *Is There a Gospel for the Rich?* Lincoln, RI: Mowbray, 1992.

Hjalmarson, Leonard. *No Home Like Place: A Christian Theology of Place.* Portland, OR: Urban Loft, 2015.

Manzo, John. "Machines, People, and Social Interaction in 'Third-Wave' Coffeehouses." *Journal of Arts and Humanities* 3, no. 8 (August 2014) 1–12.

Ministry of Housing, Communities & Local Government. "National Statistics: English Indices Deprivation 2015." September 30, 2015. Distributed by the Government Digital Service. https://www.gov.uk/government/statistics/english-indices-of-deprivation-2015/.

Morrison, Katrina. "Social Capital in the UK: May 2017." *Office of National Statistics*, May 5, 2017. https://www.ons.gov.uk/peoplepopulationandcommunity/wellbeing/bulletins/socialcapitalintheuk/may2017/.

Bibliography

Newbigin, Lesslie. *The Gospel in a Pluralist Society*. Grand Rapids, MI: Eerdmans, 1989.

Oldenburg, Ray. *Celebrating the Third Place: Inspiring Stories about the "Great Good Places" at the Heart of Our Communities*. New York: Marlowe & Company, 2001.

———. *The Great Good Place: Cafés, Coffee Shops, Bookstores, Bars, Hair Salons, and Other Hangouts at the Heart of a Community*. New York: Marlowe & Company, 1999.

Putnam, Robert D. *Bowling Alone: The Collapse and Revival of American Community*. New York: Simon & Schuster, 2001.

Strhan, Anna. *Aliens and Strangers? The Struggle for Coherence in the Everyday Lives of Evangelicals*. Oxford: Oxford University Press, 2015.

Thwaites, James. *The Church beyond the Congregation: The Strategic Role of the Church in the Postmodern Era*. Milton Keynes, UK: Paternoster, 1999.

Watts, David, et al. *Edward Jeffreys, Healing Evangelist: History, Movement, and Legacy*. Stourbridge, UK: Transformations, 2017.

Waxman, Lisa. "The Coffee Shop: Social and Physical Factors Influencing Place Attachment." *Journal of Interior Design* 31, no. 3 (May 2006) 35–53.